FAMILIES:

W9-CTI-299

Applications of Social Learning to Family Life

by
G. R. Patterson, Ph.D.

Oregon Research Institute
University of Oregon
Eugene, Oregon

Research Press Company
2612 North Mattis Avenue
Champaign, Illinois 61820

Families: Applications of Social Learning to Family Life

ISBN 0-87822-002-X

To Dr. L. Christianson, who made it possible to "see," and to my mother and Joan, the two women who taught me what to look at.

Contents

Foreword

This is not a book that proposes to explain everything that people do. Reading and putting into practice the procedures outlined here will not satisfy all of the problems that arise in your family. However, the concepts and procedures outlined here do constitute a means by which each of us, parent and child alike, can *design* and *change* many aspects of the world in which we live.

Much of man's behavior is shaped by his past as well as by his immediate experiences. An understanding of this process puts the individual in the position of partially controlling his own behavior--a position of some dignity. In fact, the present volume concerns itself with the details, the technology as it were, of how one goes about changing one's own behavior and the behavior of those living in the immediate social environment.

Living with Children and now *Families* depict a gradual evolution of this social learning technology. The first book might be thought of as a primer, in that it presents only the bare outlines of these developments. *Families*, on the other hand, describes the more recent and extensive developments.

Since publication of the first volume the author has been privileged to work with such colleagues as Roberta Ray, David Shaw, Joe Cobb, Hy Hops, and more recently, Steve Johnson and Robert Weiss. As a group we have had extensive experience in observing large numbers of normal and problem families, and each of us has immersed himself in the problem of applying the principles to assisting families who were having difficulties. The problems encountered ranged from child management to marital conflicts. While the published research reports describe the scientific outcomes of such encounters, the present volume contains the body of information that cannot be presented in scientific papers. This includes the body of our clinical experiences and the details of how one applies the procedures to his own or to a client's family.

As we learn more in these clinical experiences, this second book will be appropriately revised. It will include, in particular, the handling of specific problems most of them encountered with two- and three-year-old children. These procedures are currently being field tested (1971).

7

Section One

People as Agents of Behavior Change

This book is about the whole family—the people who live in it, what they do to each other, and how they do it. And most importantly, it outlines procedures by which families can change themselves.

Written for parents and others who have to learn how families "work," this book gives a practical application of social learning principles to problems with which we are all familiar. The general principles have been developed by such writers as Skinner,[26] Bandura and Walters,[1] and Ullmann and Krasner.[28] An earlier book, *Living with Children*, was a primer in social learning principles which emphasized their application to some child management problems. The present volume is a more detailed outline of child management procedures, and it also expands the applications to include other family members, such as adolescents and parents.

The general process by which people change is an important concept in this book. Children change over time. Grown-ups do too; however, as adults we arrange our lives so that these changes occur rather slowly. Children change their parents, just as the parents contribute to the changes in their children. The question is, "How is it done?" This book outlines, in Section I, a social learning explanation of how parents and children go about the *normal* process of changing each other. The practical procedures necessary for changing behavior are detailed in Section II, and examples of how to change a wide range of child behaviors are found throughout the book. In Section III, however, the procedures are applied to problems involved in changing the "older" members of the family, the parents and adolescents. Section IV describes the details of the application of the procedures to some extreme problems that parents may have with "aggressive" children.

If principles are to be useful, parents should be able to use them to cope with everyday problems of child management. For example, how do you go about teaching an eighteen-month-old child to eat something besides dessert? How do you teach a six-year-old child to go to bed when you ask him to? How do you teach a mother to stop nagging and scolding all the time? How do you train a father to come out from behind his newspaper? How do you negotiate with an adolescent about the use of the family car? How do you teach yourself and your spouse to stop fighting with each other? All of these problems require that we understand how to change the behavior of another person, and how we change our own behavior. In this approach it is the parents, not the professional, who are the key agents of behavior change in the family. Throughout this book, the emphasis is upon the *parent* as a behavior manager. It is the parent who is primarily responsible for deciding what behaviors he wishes to change. The parents design the means of bringing about the change, and they carry out the program.

From this point on, you will encounter an occasional sentence in which you will find a blank and a number (1) _____ . Simply write the number and what you think is an appropriate answer on lined scratch paper. The book follows the programmed instruction format, in which the main ideas are carefully broken down into small steps and arranged in logical sequence. It requires that you actively participate in the learning process by *responding* to the material rather than just passively reading the words. Writing the responses helps you remember the material. After you have written down your answer, check it with the answers provided at the bottom of the page. When you make an error, don't bother to erase your answer but simply write the correct answer beneath it. Be sure to record your own response *before* you check it against the answer.

Occasionally you will encounter a number after a name or at the end of a sentence. These numbers refer to references listed at the end of the volume. The additional material explores a given point in greater detail than is possible in a book such as this. Your local library or bookstore could assist you in obtaining the additional material.

In this introduction there were only one or two key ideas. The main notion was that parents change the behavior of children and children (1) _____ the behavior of parents. The chapter that follows presents the first tool that is needed to understand this process.

KEY IDEAS
Behavior can be changed.
Parents and children change each other's behavior.

1. change

11

one

Social Learning: Keys to Behavior Change

Mrs. S smiled at her two-year-old Cam and said, "What is this?" as she touched her hair. Cam grinned and said, "Hair," and then stood very still as he watched to see what his mother would do next. She seemed very pleased with his answer and said, "Oh my, Cam, you *are* a good rememberer. But what is this?" and she touched her nose. Cam was becoming very excited as he shouted, "Nose!" and ran to his mother, who picked him up and hugged him.

In teaching her son to use words, Mrs. S is using a process familiar to all parents--she is using a great many rewards in training him to use words. The fascinating thing about this process is that he is training his mother just as surely as she is training him--he is rewarding her for being a good teacher. Actually, they are changing each other. This process of people changing each other goes on all of the time.

We believe that much of our behavior represents the outcome of what we have *learned* from other *people*. People "teach" people. They teach each other how to talk. They teach each other how to act in specific situations. This teaching

12

process involves an amazing variety of behaviors, including *when* to smile, *what* clothes to wear, *when* to have a temper tantrum, *how* to read, when to fight, how to work, and when to kiss someone you love. These are social skills that can be learned by observing and reacting to other people. Social learning is a term that describes this process.

In the social (1) le*arning* process both persons are being changed. The changes are small but they tend to accumulate over time. The children in the classroom are altered by the teacher, but they in turn change her behavior. Parents teach their children many social skills; in the process they themselves are changed in some basic fashion by their children. We learn social behaviors from other (2) pe_____ . In interacting with others, both ourselves and the other person are changed to some degree.

Another point is necessary to consider before discussing just how this process works. It may be easy to see how we can teach other prosocial behaviors such as hugging, working, touching, or reading. However, it is also true that perfectly reasonable parents can *accidentally* teach their children all kinds of problem behaviors and not even notice that they have done it! Perfectly lovely parents teach their children to have a temper tantrum every hour! Others train their child to whine and cry each time he is asked to go to bed at night! By their behavior other parents allow their children to learn to set fires, to steal, to suck their thumbs, to take the family car whenever they like, or to live only on peanut butter sandwiches. Most parents, of course, say they *do not want* the children to do these things. However, observing what they *do* when they interact with their child often shows that this *is*, in fact, what they are teaching. One of the functions of this book is to train family members so

1. learning   2. people

13

that they understand what they are teaching each other.

The child, on the other hand, also trains his parents to nag, scold, and even spank him! These are certainly not the parent behaviors of his choice. Nevertheless, he trains his parents to display problem behaviors. Both pro-social and (3) _problem_ behaviors are taught by people closest to you.[26] Unless you learn to take the time to observe what is going on, then you simply do not understand much about yourself or the people with whom you live. In this situation the parents change each other and their children; the latter in turn change their parents, but most do not know they are being changed, nor that each person is himself an agent of change. It's the blind leading the blind.

KEY IDEAS

Social learning is concerned with how people teach people.
Over a series of interactions, both persons change.
Both pro-social and problem behaviors are learned.

3. problem

14

two

Social Reinforcers

Why people act the way they do is something all of us talk about--like the weather, though, it is something most of us really know little about. The key concept of this book is that there is a useful explanation for much of our behavior, a concept that seems, at first glance, just "too simple."

The idea is that *much* seemingly complex human behavior can be understood in terms of man's efforts to maximize rewards and to minimize pain.[26] When applied to your own life, such ideas seem overly simplified accounts of what "really goes on." For example, your salary, food, or various prizes could be thought of as "rewards." Illness and physical pain might be "punishment." But it just is not reasonable to suppose that these things have much to do with our "personalities." Money is a reward and physical pain is a punishment, but they probably have little to do, directly, with the learning of most social behaviors. The rewards and punishments which govern them are much more subtle, and also being close at hand are almost invariably overlooked by persons attempting to understand their own behavior or that of their child.

Let's begin with the general idea first and then go on to its practical implications. There are many different things that can function as a reward or a reinforcer, and they all have one thing in common. When a behavior is followed by a reinforcer, the behavior is strengthened. This means that the behavior is more likely to occur again in the future.

If you reinforce a child as soon as he finishes mowing the lawn, then he is more likely to mow the lawn again. If you forget to reinforce him, then he is less likely to do it again. Reinforcers (1) _strengthen_ behavior.

Mrs. S. placed Cam down on the floor, saying, "All right, now, ready, set, go!" Cam raced over, touched the wall, and shot back to his mother with all the speed his stubby legs could muster. She clapped her hands and with a surprised expression on her face, exclaimed, "Wow! You are back already!" No basketball star ever acknowledged the crowd's acclaim with greater nonchalance than did Cam at this point. She gave him a hug and then he stepped back expectantly as she got ready to repeat the game.

There is a great deal of reinforcement occurring here, but little of it had anything to do, directly, with the things that come to mind, when we speak of rewards. No money changed hands; no prizes were given. The reinforcers that occurred here were *social* in nature. They are to be found only in the behavior of another person. Unlike money, there is an endless supply; if you give a lot of reinforcers, you will not run out.

The first clear-cut social reinforcer in the example above was the "hand clapping" when Cam returned from his run. Then there was the

1. strengthen

16

pleased expression on his mother's face, and her saying "Wow! You are back already!" These (2) _re_____ strengthened his behaviors associated with the "game." In the future when she asks Cam to play the "ready, set, go game," he will be more likely to do it.

During the game Cam frequently ran over and hugged his mother around her legs; sometimes he would smile and laugh. These things are also social (3) _r_____ which *strengthen the mother's behavior*. Let's suppose that Cam simply marched dully through the game, not even glancing at his mother. No hugs, no smiles, no laughing countenance. By failing to reinforce his mother, he would *decrease* the likelihood that they would play such games again. If this happened very many times he would train his mother not to play with him at all.

The most powerful reinforcers for a child or an adult are found in the behaviors of another person. These are the "little things," the close attention of another person, a touch, words of approval, a smile, a glance, or a kiss. All of these behaviors are examples of (4) _social_____ reinforcers.

The beauty of these reinforcers is that they really cost nothing to give. For most people, they occur hundreds of times each day. You are being reinforced in almost every interaction that occurs during your day; you in turn are reinforcing your friends and acquaintances. If you are talking and your friend listens to you, the social reinforcer which you receive is your friend's (5)_____. When he stops listening and begins to look about the room you will probably stop talking and let him "take his turn" while you listen. If you observe closely, you will notice that there are definite traffic signals indicating when each of you is to begin and when you are to stop. Almost always there is a fair trade in that each

2. reinforcers 3. reinforcers 4. social 5. listening

of you reinforces the other at an equitable rate.[19]

There are some persons who just seem "naturally" good at reinforcing other people. They have the knack of making others glad to be around them. This _skill can be learned_. First, remember to reinforce the other person by using praise and approval occasionally. Don't be a MISER--REINFORCE ONCE IN AWHILE. In addition, pay close attention to what he is saying. Look at the other person as he talks. Some people have "roving eyes"--they simply are not a good audience. Give the other person your full attention. Touch people once in a while. Touching, smiling, and kissing are beautiful reinforcers. All of these things can be learned.

Each friend teaches you what it is that you are to talk to him about. He does this by being interested in only some of the things that you generally talk about, and not others. For some of the topics you ordinarily talk about he listens closely; for others he tends to become bored rather quickly. You train your friends and they train you. Notice that each of your friends has trained you to talk about slightly different topics. As a test of these notions, try to introduce a new topic into the conversation and note how quickly the conversation drifts back into the same old lines. Being trained to talk to a friend about things that "interest" him is a small thing. Nevertheless, in a very real sense, both you and your friend have changed each other.

A single reinforcement does not produce dramatic, long-term changes in behavior. Rather, it takes hundreds of reinforcements, consistently given, before long-term changes can be observed. For example, let's suppose you were to do the seemingly impossible and teach your wife to talk about fishing. You would have to raise the topic each night and then as soon as she began talking about it, sit back and listen attentively. You would also have to program yourself to ignore most other topics introduced by your wife. I

18

have observed a number of wives trained by such a process who find themselves in the odd position of talking night after night about their husband's work because it was the only thing in the world that would bring him out from behind his newspaper. If the wife were to receive any reinforcement at all, she had to introduce these same topics night after night.

Behavior changes; but the changes are gradual and are most likely to occur if you are consistent. If you try to teach your child to hang up his coat when he comes home in the evening, there are several things to consider. First, of course, it helps to have good models for behavior.[1] If both parents hang up their clothes, that increases the likelihood that the child might try to do the same. However, even if both parents were perfect models, it would not insure their child's being in any way similar. Excellent models mean the child will be likely to "try it too." But when he tries it, he must be (6) _____ , if the behavior is to occur consistently.

Even if both parents use the "windmill technique" of throwing their clothes into randomly selected corners, they could still teach their child to hang up his. It would be necessary only to provide a prompting cue, such as, "Please hang up your clothes." When he complies, then supply an immediate social reinforcer such as, "Thank you." This is a behavior you wish to strengthen. Remember to *notice* it when it occurs and *reinforce* it. Just one reinforcer will (7) _____ do it. Rather, it is more likely to take several weeks of consistent reinforcement on your part. Once he has learned to hang up his clothes and does it *all* of the time, *then* you can begin to slim down the reinforcement schedule. But, more about this later. Long-term changes occur slowly and primarily as a result of a great (8) _____ of social reinforcements.

6. reinforced   7. not   8. number

At this point you should track yourself as a reinforcing agent. For the next twenty-four hours note the number of times that you use such social reinforcers as "approve," "touch," "hug," or "listen attentively." Each time you do this, put down a mark by the name of the family member to whom you gave the reinforcer. At the end of the day you will have a rough notion of just how reinforcing you are and to whom you direct the reinforcers. Many parents are surprised to find that they do not tend to reinforce people, or that one person "gets it all." It is not difficult to change this, but as a first step, observe yourself and collect the data. *Observation* and *data collection* are the first steps in changing behavior.

Suppose that you find that you just do not reinforce other people very much. One thing that you might do is set up a *daily* practice session that would last for just thirty minutes. During that time, go on with your work, but every five minutes, stop what you are doing and find one thing for which you can reinforce another person. Then return to what you were doing until another five minutes have gone by.

After four or five days of such practice sessions, you should notice that other family members begin to reinforce you at a higher rate. If you give more reinforcement to others, you will receive more from them.[3] This is very much like the old Christian ethic, "You get what you give." In this case it is also one which research evidence supports. Keep in mind that these changes will come about *gradually*. You may have to do a good deal of giving before you notice any changes.

Some parents have found the dinner table to be an excellent practice situation. During the thirty minutes that the family is together, it is generally possible to give at least one reinforcer to each family member.

One interesting and very important aspect of all this is the differences in style exhibited by various people. Some people are miserly in their use of social reinforcers, and others have a kind of "sandwich approach" in which a criticism is slipped in between several reinforcers.

> The children come to the kitchen one by one and sit down at the table. Mr. C looks very closely at each of them but says nothing and begins passing the food around. The family's approach to supper is reminiscent of a group of loggers rushing through the first helping in order to get seconds, with no social amenities along the way.
>
> Mr. C breaks the silence by saying, "You came when you were called tonight, Craig. That was good." After a pause he adds, "You forgot to wash your face and hands." At this point he launches into a long lecture about Craig's being generally sloppy and ill-mannered....

While the father was *trying* to use social reinforcers, his "style" would not strengthen Craig's coming to the table when he was called. A reinforcer *must not be a sugarcoating for punishment*, which is a practice used by a surprising number of parents. If you suspect you are such a parent, you might have your spouse or even one of the children begin counting this behavior for you. The best way to begin getting control over your own behavior is to (9) c_____ it yourself or have someone else observe it for you. Do not just observe it, but *record* it as well. (10) Ob_____ and (11) rec_____ and (12) re_____ are three of the first keys to behavior change.

9. count   10. Observing   11. recording   12. reinforcing

In planning our environment some of what we want will involve strengthening new behaviors so they will occur more often. It is also true, however, that part of our problem may involve weakening already existing behaviors so they will occur less often. The question is how to do it. There are three general means of bringing this about. One way to weaken behavior is by non-reinforcement, another is by punishment, and a third is by reinforcing something which will take its place.

Suppose that you and your six-year-old have trained each other so that he has become completely helpless when getting ready for school in the morning. This same child who can take his bicycle apart and put it back together again is for some reason unable to find his shirt in the morning. Even if you put it on for him, he seems unable to button it. While later in the day he has the agility and stamina of an Olympic decathlon champion, he is listless, aimless, and complaining of sore throats and sundry aches and pains when confronted with getting ready for school He has trained his mother to "hover" in constant attendance, find his shirt, tie his shoelaces, comb his hair, and even feed him in order to get him to hurry up. By being so helpless, he forces his mother to do it for him. When she finds his clothes, dresses him, and feeds him, she is *accidentally* (13) _____ him for being helpless. On the other hand, she feels that if she doesn't do these things he will be late for school. People will label her as a bad mother. Just how does the social learning process work on a real problem like this?

First, observe for several mornings. What specific things have you been trained to do for him? Then, weaken the helpless behaviors, *and at the same time* strengthen behaviors which relate to his taking care of himself. When he does some-

13. reinforcing

thing for himself you must be certain to reinforce him, "Hey, you found your shirt; that's a big boy." To weaken the helplessness requires simply that you do not reinforce it. He may even be late for school for a few days. When this happens, arrange a consequence for being late. The "punishment" should be a natural consequence such as, "No TV at night when you have been late for school." The list of natural reinforcers which you can withdraw is very long; for example, desserts at night, the right to ride the bicycle, or the right to leave the yard after school.

When he is helpless, don't reinforce him. If this results in his being late, the punishment could be the removal of a reinforcer that he has been taking for granted.

When you begin such a program, you must remember to be consistent. If the child is occasionally in such a hurry that you feel you must help him dress and thus reinforce his helplessness, you are arranging things so that it will be even more difficult for him to change. He learns then that if he *really* acts helpless you will break down and do it for him. In this way you actually make things much worse. To be effective in weakening behavior, do not reinforce *any* of it. Reinforcing such a behavior only once in a while is actually a means of making it much stronger.[26]

Earlier it was emphasized that during the *initial* stages of strengthening a new behavior it is important to reinforce the behavior every time it occurs. However, there are *two* stages to the training. When the behavior is occurring at the rate that you wish, for example, the child dresses himself every day in time for school, then it is important to reinforce him only every other time. If he continues to work on this arrangement, then you would shift it down to reinforcing him every third time, then every fourth, and so on until it is necessary to only occasionally comment on the situation. Again, the key word is *gradual.* If his behavior is weakened or disrupted when you reduce the reinforcement, then go back and

23

reinforce him every time for a while. *His behavior tells you how fast you can move.*

When you wish to strengthen behavior, reinforce it every time at first and then gradually lessen the schedule. To weaken a behavior, *never* reinforce it. In the next chapter, we will discuss another means of weakening behavior which is somewhat more complex in the effects it has both upon you and your child.

KEY IDEAS
Reinforcers strengthen behavior.
Non-reinforcers weaken behavior.
Social reinforcers change behavior.
Social reinforcers include a smile or praise.
To change behavior, first observe it.
Then record it.

three

Aversive Stimuli: Variations on a Theme of Punishment

People can change the social environment in which they live. The social environment consists of the people with whom you live. You can change their behavior and they can change yours. One way to change the behavior of the other person is to arrange the proper reinforcers for some new behavior. You could also weaken some other behaviors by no longer reinforcing them. These two processes can be used to make *gradual* but *major* changes in your immediate social environment.

Sometimes we react as if we believe that behaviors must change *immediately*. Parents, when they punish, are indicating that things must change *right now!* Most of us have learned that rapid changes in behaviors can sometimes be brought about by using pain or punishment. In fact, some parents become trained to apply it continuously to spouses, children, and anyone else within range. In opting to produce quick changes by using punishment, they pay a certain price--as we shall presently see.

Punishment "works." If you use it properly it will produce rapid changes in the behavior of other people. If this is so, why not use it all of the time, as some people seem to do? The reason why it must be used cautiously is that there is a price tag attached. Observation of real people, in

25

real social settings, shows that the individual who gives the most reinforcement receives the most reinforcement *and* that the person in the family who gives the most punishment receives the most (1) _____ from other family members. [19]

YOU GET WHAT YOU GIVE.

There is an odd kind of equity which holds when people interact with each other. In effect, we get what we give, both in amount and in kind. Each of us seems to have his own bookkeeping system for love, and for pain. Over time, the books are balanced, as shown in a number of studies actually observing what it is that people do with each other.[19]

If the mother yells and screams at the children, they will find ways of punishing her in return. Observation studies do show that mothers who yell and scold a lot have children who do the same. In some families the child may pay his mother back by stealing from her purse. Or, the husband who shouts at his wife may find that his meals are poorly prepared.

The price for using aversive stimuli to control behavior is that they will be returned in amount and perhaps in kind. In a family, the person who does the most punishing will receive the (2) _____ punishment from others. The whole family can become very busy playing the endless game of "getting even." For this reason, punishment should be used sparingly, if at all.

When people think of punishment occurring in a family, they ordinarily think of scolding, yelling, and spanking because these are the things which occur most often. However, a surprising number of parents use hitting as a means of punishing the child. They wait until the child's behavior is absolutely intolerable to them and then rush in, hitting to the right and left in a desperate attempt to get things calmed down. In one sense this "works." After the hitting, things are usually

1. punishment   2. most

pretty quiet *for a short time.* The noise and clamor subside. This reinforces the parents for hitting. The next time the children get into a noisy hassle the parents are more likely to resort to hitting again. When the parents scold or hit, the children will stop being disruptive for a few minutes, which reinforces the parents for (3) _____ or (4)_____ . In this manner the children *train parents* to scold and yell a good part of the day. Parents who scold and hit are not "bad" people or "sick" people. They have simply allowed their (5) _____ to train them to do things they really don't want to be doing.

The children's hassling seldom slows down for more than a few moments after a scolding; and many parents find themselves caught up in an endless cycle of the children's fighting, followed by their nagging, with this followed by a brief period of quiet, and then a repetition of the whole episode.

There *are* some kinds of punishment that do work. But most parents do not make use of them; instead they persist in allowing their children to teach them to use the *wrong* punishment at the *wrong* time.

Mrs. W is working in the kitchen getting supper ready for her four children. In the next room, the noise level has been steadily building for the past few moments. One of the children runs into the kitchen, "Momma, Sherry took my doll." Sherry comes bouncing into the room laughing, "Your doll is behind the stove." Mrs. W says to the younger sister, "Momma's busy, you go and play. Sherry, you behave

3. scolding   4. hitting   5. children

yourself." Shortly after the two children leave the room, there is a resounding crash and the young infant breaks into a piercing cry. Mrs. W runs into the next room and is greeted with Sherry shouting, "I didn't do it, Mommy! She fell off the chair!" Without breaking her stride, Mrs. W strikes Sherry, pushing her aside, and runs to her baby. The infant is not seriously injured but now Sherry is crying as well and the mother is shouting at all of the children in the room.

She waited too long. There was a five- or ten-minute period in which the children were becoming increasingly out of control. It should have been possible to interfere with the "build-up" by sending one or more children outside or bringing one of them into the kitchen to help her. By doing either of these things she would be using a *mild* form of punishment (removal from the group) and heading off the trouble before it really began.

In this family, Sherry is the instigator--she indiscriminately teases her sisters, her mother, the dog, the cat, and even her grandmother whenever Grandma has the courage to visit. The mother could have applied a mild punishment when it became reasonably clear that Sherry was teasing her younger sister. She could have used Time Out, the details of which we will go into later. Essentially, Time Out means removing Sherry from all of that reinforcement she was getting by teasing and sending her to the bathroom for five minutes. She could also have said, "You were teasing, that means no dessert for you tonight." In this situation there is *no* scolding, i.e., she did *not* say, "You are a bad girl," nor did she scream, "Sher--ry! Stop that!"

If you decide to use punishment, *stay calm.* Use something mildly aversive, but do it *every time.* Catch the problem at its beginning, then use some mildly aversive natural consequence.

It is amazingly difficult to use a mild consequence (6) _____ time the problem behavior occurs. Most of us would simply rather not bother. DO IT NOW. DO IT EVERY TIME. Most parents find that it helps them to be consistent in handling such a problem by using the observation and recording procedures described in a later chapter. To really change such a behavior you must set aside a week or two in which you *carefully* track the behavior and consistently react when it occurs. Furthermore, when using even moderate punishments you should increase the amount of reinforcement which the child is receiving for pro-social behavior. For example, you might make it a point to reinforce him for a set of behaviors which would compete with "teasing." Each time Mrs. W sees Sherry playing well with one of her sisters, she should go over and say, "Hey, that's really nice. You two are playing so quietly I hardly knew you were here. What are you doing?" A few moments' participation would be a powerful (7) _____ for Sherry's play with siblings. When using mildly punishing consequences to (8) we_____ a problem behavior, also plan to use reinforcement to strengthen some set of behaviors that will take its place.

Changing behavior requires that you have a plan or a program and that you follow it for a week or two. To be consistent in reinforcing some behavior and ignoring or punishing others, it is necessary to collect and record your observations. Just "making up your mind" is not sufficient for most parents, particularly when they are first learning.

6. every, each   7. reinforcer   8. weaken

HOMEWORK

Count the number of critical comments, scolds, disagreements, lectures, and nags you deliver to one member of the family over a five-day period. Each time one occurs, make a mark on a piece of paper that you keep handy. This kind of recordkeeping will also alert you to errors in "timing." You should begin to notice whether you tend to wait too long and how consistent you are. It will probably turn out that you are a "random nagger," that is, for the same behavior sometimes you nag and sometimes you don't.

KEY IDEAS

You get what you give.
To get more reinforcement--give more.
To get less punishment--give less.
Intervene early.
Use mildly aversive consequences.
Use the aversive consequences EVERY time.
Remain calm.
Set up a program where you also reinforce some competing behaviors.

four

How to Do It:
Precision Reinforcement

The ability to use social reinforcers to change behavior is a skill possessed by very few people, and one that is somewhat analogous to skill in using the English language. Everyone does it hundreds of times each day, but few of us do it well. Your ability to help your child change his behavior, and have the change persist, will depend largely upon your ability to practice the *skills outlined in this chapter. None* of the ideas presented here will be unfamiliar to you. Not one of the ideas is too complicated for a five-year-old child to understand. However, most people put them into practice so haphazardly that they come to feel that it is impossible to change the behavior of other people.

The first concept to be emphasized is that when you see a behavior that you like, *reinforce* it. Many parents notice when the child does something which they especially like, but say that if they indicate their approval it will "spoil" the child. This is probably just an excuse. Such a "sphinx parent" seldom reinforces anyone. He believes that the child ought to behave because that is what children are supposed to do. In our experience, sphinx parents can change and thus become more effective parents.

At the other extreme is the "gusher," who hugs, caresses, praises, and attends *no matter what the child does.* It is not that he "loves too much," but that he (1) <u>re</u>_____ the child no matter what he does. A good behavior manager reinforces immediately when desirable behavior occurs. *If* the child behaves, *then* reinforce him. If not, then ignore the behavior. The latter, if used over a long period of time will (2) _____ the undesirable behavior.

At this point we are assuming that you are attempting to teach the child to do something regularly that he does only once in a while. For example, many parents complain. "He never talks to us."

Harold comes in from school, walks into the kitchen, "Hi, Mom," and peers into the refrigerator. His mother, in the middle of preparing supper, hardly looks up as she says, "How was it today?" He stands looking at a magazine, absent-mindedly paging through it as he munches. "We had a race at school today for some guys who came to see how fast we were." Mother, by now deep in her casserole, says, from a great distance, "That's nice," at which point Harold goes into the other room.

Actually, Harold won that race and was clearly the fastest runner in the third grade, as his mother discovered later. He could have said that he had won an Olympic gold medal and still received only a mumbled, "That's nice," as a reinforcer. The point is that he talked and she did (3) _____ reinforce him effectively. If you occasionally miss supporting a pro-social behavior, it is no great matter. But if you miss all

1. reinforces   2. weaken   3. not

of the time, then your Harold will simply stop giving you that behavior.

IF YOU LIKE IT, REINFORCE IT.

Reinforcing Harold would require only that the mother listen to him attentively for a few moments and ask him about his race. She might actually stop working for a few moments but that is probably not necessary. What *is* required is that she listen carefully to what he is saying. When he talks, she (4) _____ . In doing this, she is providing the immediate reinforcement that is required to strengthen a behavior. If she reinforces him in this way for talking about school, he will, in the future, be more likely to (5) t_____ . During the early stages of training she should reinforce him (6)_____ time he attempts to describe things going on in his life.

Thus far we have made two points. When attempting to strengthen a behavior, reinforce it (7) _____ and do it (8) _____ time. Even after the child has learned to regularly engage in the new behavior, you should never take the behavior for granted. If you like what he is doing, (9) _____ him for it.

It would be difficult to overemphasize the importance of reinforcing *immediately*. The longer you wait, the less likely it is to be effective. For example, one mother waits until after supper to tell her daughter that she appreciated her hanging up her coat. A second parent reinforces her son a few seconds after he hangs up his coat. The child most likely to hang up his coat in the future would be the one who was reinforced after a (10) _____ _____ . Don't wait. Do it now.

If the words "immediate" and "often" summarize the first two points made in this chapter, the phrase "small steps" would best characterize

4. listens   5. talk   6. every   7. immediately
8. every   9. reinforce   10. few seconds

33

the third. This too requires real artistry. Again, the problem is to strengthen a behavior that does not occur or one that occurs very seldom. For example, how *do* you really teach a child to "be a good student," to "talk to me," to "be more polite," or to "be more assertive"? If you were to wait until your child gets all B's on his report card to reinforce him, *it would never happen.* This is a very complex behavior with literally *hundreds* of small steps required to reach a goal. But those small steps are the points along the way where you can reinforce him. If you plan to wait until he is President of the United States before you reinforce him, he may not even learn to tie his shoes.

Some parents behave as if using reinforcers "wears them out," or as if it will spoil the child. It isn't *too much* love that spoils a child; it is being reinforced for the wrong behaviors.

Reinforce him for starting and then for each step along the way. This process is called "shaping." It consists of two steps. First decide just what it is that you wish to bring about. Second, decide on the steps necessary to arrive at this point and break them down into *very* small units. Let's take as an example the goal of "being a good student" for a boy who consistently earns less than a D average. The teachers say that he could do much better work. What kind of grades *would* it be reasonable to aim for as a goal for your training program?

Begin with a rather modest goal of, say, a C average. Next, think of just what your child would have to do to earn a C average; for example, completing more of his homework assignments. Maybe he should begin studying *early* in the term; perhaps he needs a consistent study program. These are vague goals, though, and they do not constitute a description of a program.

If an average child studies one hour a day, five days a week at the start of the term, he should be able to earn at least a C average. *Now* you have a specific goal--teach him to study an hour a day. Notice, the word is *teach*, not *force*. Next, you must decide where and when the training will take place. Select a quiet place in your home, perhaps his room, where he is to study. Then, after discussing it with him, set a time most convenient for him and the rest of the family; for example, right after supper and *before* the TV set is turned on is often a good time.

A good student may study an hour a day. However, for someone who does not study at all, an hour a day is an *enormous* step. If he tries it, it will almost certainly be painful to him and he probably will not use the time well. TAKE A SMALLER STEP. In fact, begin where he is now. If he actually studies (on the average) about five minutes a day, begin there.

On the first day, he studies five minutes in his room AND THEN HE GETS REINFORCED. DO NOT TEST HIM to find out if he really studied. For some children, just sitting still for five minutes might be an adequate first step.

The reinforcer may be praise from you. Or, perhaps he must study five minutes to *earn* a natural consequence, such as the right to watch TV that night. No studying, no TV. There are many kinds of reinforcers that could be used; and some of them will be discussed in a later chapter. For the moment, it is important to emphasize that your program begins where the child's skills are. Set up the beginning of the program so that he is almost certain to earn a (11) _____. Gradually increase the size of the steps. After the second or third day you might set the study timer (a kitchen timer will do nicely) at ten minutes. Increase the steps only when you are reasonably sure that he can stay in there (and work) for that period of time. If ten minutes is too long, then go back to five minutes for a while. Keep the steps within his range.

11. reinforcer

If things break down, then your steps are too (12) _____ . It may also be that the reinforcers are too weak. Change your program. If he stops studying it does not mean that he is a bad boy or a "hopeless case." It simply means that *you* have to change the (13) _____ .

As he goes along, increase the requirements so that he must do more work in order to earn the same reinforcers. By the end of a week or two he may be studying fifteen or twenty minutes each evening. For some children, talking to him about his work *might* be a powerful reinforcer. That does not mean a quiz session in which you try to decide whether he really knows the material. Do not nag him about his work. *Do not punish him for performance that is not perfect*. Rather, your role is to reinforce him for slow gradual development of skills that will lead to a C grade.

Bill comes out of his room after his study session and puts his books on the kitchen table. His father looks up from reading the paper. "There is the clock watcher now. How did it go?" Bill just replies, "OK," as he goes toward the TV set. The father has put down his paper. "Well, how about letting me take a look at what you have been doing?" Bill looks dejected; apparently he has been through this many times before. The father takes the essay that Bill was working on, "Get this all done tonight?" Bill nods. "My god, it is messy. Why don't you use an eraser? Hey, what kind of spelling do they teach you kids nowadays? How do you spell...." And the inquisition goes on...and on....

12. big, large   13. program, reinforcers, steps

This is *not* a good example of a parent reinforcing a child for the first steps in a study program. Rather, it is a good example of a father using (14) pu_____ for behaviors that fail to be perfect. Bill DOESN'T HAVE TO BECOME PRESIDENT IN ORDER TO EARN A REINFORCER. The result of such a training program will be that Bill simply stops engaging in the study behavior at all. The father will report that he used small steps and social reinforcers but the program did not work. The error lay in the father's use of (15)_____. Punishment almost always (16)_____ the response that it follows. This father, in his role of "prosecuting attorney," is training the boy to (17)_____ studying. He is actually working against the goal which he has set--to help his son study.

One alternative to all of this emphasis upon specific goals, small steps, lots of reinforcement, and no punishment is to offer a BRIBE. A bribe usually means offering a large reward to get someone to do something that is illegal. There is another sense in which some parents use a bribe. This parent seldom reinforces pro-social behaviors; therefore his training programs for the child have been so sloppy that he can't be *sure* of what the child is going to do next. So he uses a bribe, "If you are a good boy and don't tease, or fight for the whole week that your grandmother is here, we will give you a dollar." Nothing illegal about it. The underachieving student is often bribed, "I'll give you five dollars for every A that you get," or "I'll give you a dollar for every C that you get." The problem with using bribes is not a novel one at all. It is the simple fact that these kinds of bribes often do not work. As used by most parents, bribes are an inept use of a reward to cover up the fact that they have done a sloppy job of training the child.

14. punishment   15. punishment   16. weakens   17. stop

In the example above, the child was told that he would be "reinforced" for studying, or for being good. *That* is good. He was also told the specific goal is for him to get an A or a C or to play with his sister without teasing and fighting. Those goals were somewhat vague. Practically speaking, the "programs" were sloppy because, for many children, the steps required to reach the goal were too large and/or not clearly specified. *How* do you get an A, anyway?

The child *might* work out a study program on his own, but why leave things to chance? If the child does happen to work out a study program, would the parent-briber remember to reinforce him each day for making a step at a time? Probably not; such a parent would feel that it is easier to dole out the five dollars at the end of the whole series of steps. Parents who use bribes don't have to feel responsible; they can always say that they "tried." If the bribe fails, it is the child's fault; the parent did his "duty." The bribe is usually a *substitute* for the parents' *planning* a program and *participating* in it every day. If the child's behavior is important, it deserves your careful planning and participation. Anything worth doing deserves something better than a bribe.

If a planned program does not work, any one of three things may be involved. The (18)_____ may be too large. The (19) _____ may be too weak, or you might be mixing in a good deal of (20) _____ while you reinforce the child. Sit down and talk to the child about what you are trying to do and *let him* help you design a better program. If the child's behavior is not changing, it is *not his fault;* it is just a bad program. Keep changing it until it works.

18. steps   19. reinforcer, reinforcement
20. punishment, nagging, criticism

The concept of shaping is so crucial that it might be helpful to work through one more example. This time we will work with the problem of thumb-sucking in a four-year-old child. After observing that during the hour before bedtime he has his thumb in his mouth an average of about thirty-five minutes, the parents have planned a program. Their observations show that he is fairly consistent over two or three days. They are now ready to begin a program; they give him the following explanation:

> "Tim, you say you want to stop sucking your thumb. It does seem hard for you to stop. Well, we are going to help you practice not sucking your thumb. I think it will be fun for you. Practice time will be just before you go to bed. If you can go for five minutes without putting your thumb in your mouth, you get to put a mark here on this card on the refrigerator" (shows him). "When you get ten marks, you and I will take a special trip to the zoo, just for you. I will set the kitchen timer so we will know when five minutes have gone by. Let's practice now to see how this works. Ready? Remember, do not put your thumb in your mouth and you earn one mark."

There are many ways of using "marks," and we will return to this technique in a later chapter. But for now, the instructions should be clear, specific, and with the least amount of implied criticism or subtle nagging. Emphasize that it will be fun for him, as indeed it will when it comes time to put the mark on his "chart" on the refrigerator. If he is not successful on the first trial, label the behavior for him. "Oh, oh. You forgot and put it in your mouth. Let's try again, you goofed that one." Reset the timer but *do not nag or scold*. Keep the learning situation as pleasant and reinforcing as you can. When he goes the whole five minutes, then reinforce him, "Hey, you made it that time. No thumb in the mouth at all. That is really big boy stuff. Let's put a mark on your chart." If he then goes on and gets another five-minute block, you might increase the time interval to seven or eight minutes.

Mention your pleasure at his successful practice at other times during the day. One of the best reinforcers is to "brag about him" when a friend drops by and he "happens" to be in earshot. "Tim is really working on not sucking his thumb; today he went for almost a whole hour without even sucking his thumb once. He is really becoming a big boy."

If you notice at any time during the day that he does not have his thumb in his mouth, you should reinforce him. "Hey, there is no thumb in your mouth." Announce his successes at the family dinner table and encourage the other members to reinforce him. These programs are all-out efforts and for best results should involve as many of the family as possible.

Each day the time intervals should be increased so that eventually his "step" is a full hour to earn one mark. You might then increase the time interval to several hours. At the end of two to three weeks, the effects should carry over to other times of the day and the program could be gradually phased out. This means that the time required to earn a mark has become large (a day); by this time the marks themselves may have become reinforcers. Later, when you think he is ready, ask him if he thinks you could drop the record-keeping. He may decide to keep his own records, as some professional scholars do. If his progress is maintained, you then might also consider reducing your schedule of marks and use only social reinforcers. However, to be main-

40

tained, his behavior must be (21)_____
once in a while.

The thumb-sucking is likely to recur from time to time. For example, when grandmother comes to visit, the thumb may return to its resting place. You might then explain the program to her and use some sections of it for a day or two. Programs are family affairs. Simply re-introduce some, or all, of the old program until the behavior disappears again.

In summary, discuss with the child what it is that you are trying to do. Tell him you are going to work *together* on a problem that has been difficult for him to handle. Use as little (22)_____ as possible. Have a specific goal in mind. Begin the program at such a level that he is *bound* to receive an immediate (23)_____ .

As he moves along, increase the size of the steps. If at all possible, involve several members of the (24)_____ as *reinforcers (not* as spies). When the behavior is under control, gradually fade out the program. Be prepared for an occasional burst of the old problem behavior.

HOMEWORK

For a three-day period record the number of social reinforcers you use with your children. Select a one-hour period--the same one each day; for example, five to six p.m. Record, on *paper* the total for each day.

After this baseline period, practice each day for a week doubling the number of reinforcers. KEEP A RECORD EACH DAY. This may seem very artificial at first, but after a few days of practice it will become quite natural. Your skill as a social reinforcer is one of the keys to the success of the programs you introduce. Touch your children

21. reinforced   22. punishment, criticism, nagging
23. reinforcement   24. family

and spouse, kiss them, or praise them. Try to make
the reinforcers contingent upon behaviors that you
particularly value.

KEY IDEAS
Reinforce immediately and often.
To be consistent, set up a program including:
>   specific goal
>   specific steps
>   small steps.
Begin where the child is.
Involve the family.
If the behavior does not change, it is a bad program, not a bad
child.

five

What Kind of Reinforcers?

Probably the most available, useful, and important consequences are those such as praise, touch, attention, and smiles. These are simple things. They occur hundreds of times each day and for each of us they are provided by a large number of people.

If any one of these social reinforcers consistently follows a child's behavior, then that behavior is likely to occur again in the future. Most new behaviors are probably learned by the process of the child's first observing others and then trying it out himself.[1, 26] If he receives social reinforcers for his performance, then he is likely to try it again. If you remember to reinforce this new behavior each time it occurs for several days or weeks, then the behavior should become quite reliable. However, behavior changes so slowly that many parents tend to give up trying to produce changes this way. There is also another problem; a review of research studies suggests that some problem children are less responsive to social reinforcers given by adults.[9, 29] This means that parents of problem boys who rely *only* upon social reinforcers may have to work that much harder to produce changes.

For these reasons, it is sometimes necessary to consider other ways to initially increase the effectiveness of parental management, such as non-social reinforcers. Used together with social reinforcers, they usually bring about very rapid changes in behavior.

Many of the non-social reinforcers which occur are taken for granted; for example, the morning coffee break, the daily dessert after dinner, watching TV, and playing golf. For a child, non-social reinforcers include such things as riding his bike, playing outside in the yard with friends, reading comics, or having no chores to do. These prosaic things can be used as powerful reinforcers.

L. Homme [4] showed that the key to proper usage of non-social reinforcers lies in the skill with which one arranges the "contingency contract." *First*, specify the behavior to be strengthened, i.e., "a little bit of studying," *and then* provide the non-social reinforcer, "watching TV." In such an agreement, his study behaviors can actually be strengthened. This "first-and-then" principle has been shown by researchers such as Homme to have many practical possibilities for parents and teachers. For example, when you come home, *first* talk to your wife for a few minutes *and then* read the paper. *First* your child hangs up his coat *and then* he gets his after-school snack. (1) _____ he washes his face, and then he eats supper. First he eats his peas and corn, and (2) _____ he gets his dessert.

The first-and-then notion uses readily available *natural consequences;* it requires only a little imagination to identify consequences appropriate for you and for your child. They all have certain things in common. They occur often, at least once a day, and we tend to take them for granted. In contingency management we simply make it necessary to earn the good things in life. You give up the "right" to read the paper and agree to earn it by talking to your wife. As

1. First   2. then

another example, you might "earn" the right to sit down at the dinner table by first requiring that you weigh yourself.

Take a "weak" behavior that seldom occurs, and require that it be performed *before* you have access to one of these non-social reinforcers that you take for granted. Contingency management requires only that you identify natural consequences which occur regularly and specify the manner in which they are to be earned.

For children such arrangements can be facilitated by setting up a contract (details will be covered in a later chapter). A contract lists the *specific* things which the child may do and the number of points earned for each. The points are recorded each day so the child can observe his own progress. When he gets a specified number he earns some natural consequence which he values very much. For example, twenty points might earn a trip to the bowling alley with father, a Saturday afternoon movie, a model airplane, or a streamer for his bike. The points and the back-up reinforcer are negotiated with the child beforehand so that he understands exactly what the "game" is.

"Jane, you do lots of nice things around here but your room is still pretty messy. Nagging you every day about it doesn't work; besides, neither you nor I like that very much anyway. I have an idea about how to teach you to keep your room clean. I think it will be fun for you and also I won't have to nag you about it anymore.

"The way this game works is that you get a chance to earn something that you really want at the same time that you are learning to keep your room neat and picked up. Interested? OK. Here is the way it works. Each morning I check to see if you have made your bed and put away your clothes and toys. If all three things have been done, you get a point for that day; I mark it right here on this card."

Jane's Point Card for August 10-16

M	T	W	T	F	S	S

If the bed is made *and* the clothes and toys put away, she gets one point in the morning and another after supper. When she gets 10 points, she earns _____ .

"We will tape the card to the refrigerator so you can see it each day. What would you like to earn with your ten points? ...No, a new bike is too expensive; pick something else. How about having Sally come and stay overnight for a pajama party? ...OK, that is what we will do this week, and you might think of what you want to earn for next week."

Each point the mother records is a nonsocial (3) _____ for the child's keeping her room picked up. Naturally, the mother will *also* use (4) _____ reinforcers to further strengthen the behavior.

Do not require that the room be perfect on the first day. If the bed was sloppily made, but an obvious attempt was made, *give her the point.*

3. reinforcer   4. social

You might suggest that if she can make it perfectly she will get two points. Model it for her and *show her* what you mean. Then, tear the bed up and have her try to reproduce what it is that you want. In this way you are *being specific*. She can literally see what it is that you want. Give her two points if she gets it correct during practice. *Don't be stingy with points or with social reinforcers.*

Do not debate with the child. Explain that you found some socks on the floor, so she received no point for that morning. Do not accept excuses. No Supreme Court defense on your part is required. Your arguing will reinforce her for initiating arguments in the future. If you forgot to put a mark down, or if she should have had two marks and you gave only one, *apologize* for it.

Whether you are using a contingency contract for the child to immediately earn a natural consequence or a point system which specifies a consequence to be earned several days hence, it is wise to write it down.

BE FAIR, but above all, BE REINFORCING.

Encourage the child to select her own back-up (5) _____. Also remember to select an initial level of performance that is appropriate for the child to insure her earning reinforcement during the very first stages. Do not scold or criticize; simply (6) _____ those behaviors which are appropriate. Keep the steps (7) _____ and specific. As the behavior comes under control you might increase the amount of work or the standards of performance, but discuss these increases with the child, *always* within the context of how well she is doing at the present time.

5. reinforcer, consequence   6. reinforce, strengthen
7. small

KEY IDEAS

The "first-and-then" principle makes use of natural consequences that occur every day.

Points and contracts can be used to earn natural consequences
which happen infrequently.

Be specific.

Negotiate the agreements with the child.

Be sure the child is reinforced from the very beginning.

Do not nag or scold. Wait for the pro-social behavior to occur
and then reinforce it.

six
Accidental Training

It is a paradox, but nonetheless true, that sometimes we create reinforcement arrangements such that our close friends, members of our families and others whom we love become trained to display high rates of problem behaviors! We also set up reinforcements that strengthen problem behavior in ourselves. While *unplanned*, such programs are nevertheless extremely effective. There are a number of these situations which occur frequently enough to merit discussion.

ACCIDENTALLY WITH LOVE

"How are you ever going to get to be a big, strong man if you don't eat?" Timmy, a large, corpulent eight-year-old, sits staring down at his plate heaped with food that his mother has placed in front of him. "But I don't really want all that, Ma." "You shouldn't have had a snack when you came home today. When your mama goes to all that work getting a big supper you should eat. Tell him, Herman, that he should eat." With a sigh Timmy picks up his fork. "That's a good boy. Your mama loves you."

When you go to someone's home for dinner there is a good deal of pressure for you to over-eat. Aside from praising her cooking, the primary reinforcer given the hostess is your asking for seconds. In order to reinforce her, you overeat. Similarly, in many homes the reinforcer for the mother is to have *everyone* eat as if they were preparing for a snowshoe trip into the arctic wasteland. The mother reinforces her child for strenuous overeating and then attributes his over-weight to the fact that his Uncle Charlie was fat. If he does not overeat, she punishes him. When he stuffs himself, she reinforces him. We see many problems of overweight in children as being due to accidental training by well-meaning parents. In the example above, the mother nags until he overeats and then (1) _____ him for overeating. This combination of reinforcement and (2)_____ is very effective.

In another kind of home the parents provide social reinforcers for the child's performing as an entertainer. He may be largely ignored unless he behaves like a clown or a buffoon. At this point his family becomes involved and interested, rein-forcing him at a high rate for doing and saying silly things. "Isn't he cute? Look at the way he makes a face. He'll be on TV someday."

When visitors arrive the parents prompt the child to get him started and then reinforce him when he performs. This is not to say that "clown" is a terribly deviant set of behaviors to have in one's list of skills. It becomes a problem if it is his *only* means of turning on his parents or of relating to others. For example, are they as reinforcing to him when he wishes to discuss an idea that he has or a book he has read?

A more typical example of accidental train-ing for problem behaviors is found in the system-atic programs for training in helplessness and im-maturity. This is such a frequent problem in

1. reinforces   2. punishment, criticism

50

"normal" families that programs are described in later chapters for altering these behaviors. However, there are a number of variations on this theme. In the most common one, the mother reinforces the child when he behaves in a helpless fashion. The father may also punish him for being less than perfect when he does attempt to behave in a grown-up manner.

As the father sits down to supper, Scot, the six-year-old, reaches over and takes a piece of bread and begins putting butter on it. The butter is a little hard and doesn't spread well. He begins to whine and his mother interrupts what she was saying to her husband, "Oh, here, let me do it," she says in an exasperated tone. She talks to her husband as she butters Scot's bread and then also cuts the meat on his plate into small, bite-sized chunks.

He whined and acted helpless, so she did it *for him*. In this situation, when he (3) _____ , he was reinforced. Apparently it is easier for her to do it for him than to train him to do it for himself. In itself, this is indeed a small thing, but repeat this scene in a dozen different settings each day and you have a training program in which a boy is being reinforced for helplessness. If he says that he wants to go down the street half a block to the neighbor's, his mother goes with him. When he has difficulty tying his shoes in the morning, she (4)_____ them for him. She does this because she believes it is quicker than taking the time to teach him how to *tie his own shoes.*

3. whined   4. ties

If he does attempt to tie his shoes, his father is likely to remark, "My god, look at that kid; he can't even do that right." He is punished for trying to develop skills. He gets reinforced for remaining (5) h_____ . No chores are arranged for such a child because it is "easier" for the parents to do them themselves. The child is seldom given the opportunity for developing skills, and thus gets little support for learning new competencies. As suggested by M. Ebner,[2] this child really is a "trained incompetent."

The odd thing is that many of these parents report that they do not like helpless behaviors. They simply *drifted* into this type of training program because they did not wish to take the time to plan programs for skill training.

ACCIDENTALLY AVERSIVE--
HOW TO CREATE A MONSTER

The second kind of accidental training is done with pain and punishment; it is equally effective in training adults and children. Typically, the behavior changes slowly enough over time so that neither party is aware of the changes in behavior.

The general principle involved was covered earlier; whatever turns off something painful is strengthened. When the TV set is turned up too high and your yelling leads someone to turn it down, then you were reinforced for (6) _____ . In effect, yelling "worked"; it reduced the pain. A response that was reinforced is more likely to occur again in the (7)_____ .

Noise coming from the two younger brothers playing in the living room usually leads to a remark such as, "Hey! Stop that fighting in there

5. helpless   6. yelling   7. future

or you will both get a spanking!" Usually the boys will quiet down for a few minutes. The noise or "pain" is reduced, so you get reinforced for yelling and making threats. If your children are noisy very often, they could teach you to do a lot of yelling. In this situation, the children are training the (8) _____ .

Things that make it possible for you to *avoid* pain are reinforcing. "Forgetting" to keep an appointment with the dentist is reinforcing. Bowling with friends is reinforcing. It could be doubly reinforcing if the family has trained the wife to be a nag. She in turn has trained her husband and children to stay out of the house. There is a paradox here because the family probably does not want her to be a nag and she, in turn, does not really want her husband or children to be out of the home so much. However, the wife drifts into "nagging" and the husband into "running away from home." Both behaviors work in terms of temporarily shutting off painful stimuli.

Children are involved in similar ways. If the younger sister has a comic that her brothers want to look at, they may ask for it; if she refuses, they may simply hit her and take it away. In this instance "hitting" and "taking" are reinforced because "they work." The child learns that he doesn't have to wait; whenever some other member of the family presents him with a minor pain such as teasing, yelling, or noncompliance, he can turn them off immediately by hitting. He gets paid off for hitting.

If parents do not carefully track teasing and hitting, it is very easy for one or more of the children to learn to become a first-class monster. This kind of training goes on frequently in many homes[19] and nursery schools.[1] In this kind of accidental training, the victim's being hit provides the (9) _____ that strengthens the hitting

8. parents   9. reinforcement

behavior. Nagging works because it temporarily reduces the noise; hitting is reinforced because it helps the hitter change things which are unpleasant for him. He doesn't *have* to learn how to teach his little brother to make less noise; he can hit him and turn it off immediately. He doesn't *have* to do chores; his temper tantrums will teach his (10) p_____ to stop asking him to do things.

In a great many of the families with whom we have worked, *all* of the members spend a great deal of time yelling, hitting, and punishing each other. In fact, observations in homes suggest that many otherwise quite "normal" families drift into patterns of this type. Because the pattern is so common in both normal and in problem families, Section IV will outline the steps involved in changing children's aggressive behaviors.

You are responsible for the social environment in which you live. If you don't like it, then (11) _____ it. If there are some things about it that you like, then begin tracking what other people are doing that please you and (12) _____ them when they occur. Do not take good things for granted, and do not feel that you have to put up with annoying or unpleasant behaviors either. It's your world. Observe it. And observe yourself to see what it is you are doing that makes it the way it is.

10. parents   11. change   12. reinforce

KEY IDEAS

It is easy to slip into a pattern of accidentally reinforcing problem behavior.

If problem behavior occurs in your family, observe it and see what the reinforcers might be for that behavior.

Behaviors that turn off painful stimuli are strengthened.

Nagging and scolding get strengthened because they have a short-term effect in reducing noise and other painful stimuli.

Hitting, temper tantrums, and other aggressive behaviors are reinforced by the victim.

You make your own social environment.

Section Two

Behavior Management Skills

The previous section on social learning gave some general notions on how behavior works and how it can be changed. It is not, of course, a complete theory of human behavior, but we don't think that a theory has to be able to explain everything in order for it to be useful. As it stands right now, we *can* use it to change much of our social environment.

Understanding general notions or principles is not enough. It is also necessary to understand *and* practice the procedures for putting these notions to work. This next section outlines the practical skills that must be mastered before you can be effective in changing behavior; we call these procedures "behavior management skills." We now move from "theory" to practice.

The ideas about how to make these principles work have evolved gradually as a result of our past seven years of experience in working with families who have had problem children. [13] As the parents tried to put these social learning principles into practice, certain difficulties were encountered. The efforts of numerous investigators to meet such difficulties led to the development of what might now be called "behavior management skills." In retrospect, these skills can be found in many well-run homes and nursery schools that are managed by adults who do these things quite "naturally." In some respects, the contribution of the last decade's work may amount to little more than underlining what it was that some of our wives, mothers, and grandparents did that was so effective in training children. Observation data collected in the families in the last decade helped us to understand which of these practices are crucial to good child management and which are not. The point is that *these skills can be taught to parents*. We believe that parents of normal children can profit from practicing these skills. Quite possibly practicing these management skills will alleviate some severe child management problems. However, when applying the procedures to children with severe problems of longstanding, it would be wise to seek supervision from a trained behavior modifier. Similarly, the material relating to negotiating for behavior change with adults is intended to be useful in assisting adults to live in peaceful coexistence. However, it would be wishful thinking to believe that merely reading about these procedures could change longstanding, severe marital problems.

seven

Setting Up a Management Program

RETRAINING

This section is a very brief review of the key notions scattered throughout the previous chapters. These concepts relate *directly* to the problem of behavior management skills.

When considering a training program, remember to keep track of, and plan for, the changes in *two* responses. One response consists of the problem behavior that you wish to weaken. The other is the pro-social behavior that will take its place. Arrange a program that will (1)_____ the problem behavior and (2)_____ the pro-social behavior.

First (3)_____ and count each of the behaviors. Notice the reinforcing arrangements for each that exist within the family.

Second, plan a program that specifies the goal you wish to achieve.

Third, specify the steps required to get there. A good program will lay out the *many* small steps required to produce the terminal behavior; it will also include the reinforcers needed to strengthen the new behaviors. During the early stages of the program (4) _____ small

1. weaken   2. strengthen   3. observe   4. every

59

step is reinforced (5) _____ . The program should also spell out the arrangements used to weaken the problem behavior. These arrangements, if used at all, should stress non-reinforcement or Time Out as the principal means of weakening behavior. Do not use physical (6)_____ , nagging, or criticism.

Behaviors do not change in one day or even one week. Many of them may require several weeks before the data show clear changes. The observation data help you to keep track of just what the changes are; if they show that the behavior hasn't altered, then CHANGE THE PROGRAM. The steps may be too large, the reinforcers too (7)_____ or too few. Perhaps you are not being consistent; some problem behaviors may get reinforced. Perhaps you are not giving social reinforcers or points *each time* the new behaviors occur. Perhaps you mix your arrangements so that the child is receiving *both* positive reinforcers *and* punishment for the new behaviors. If the child's behavior does not change, it means that you and your program must change.

As you go along you should plan on involving other family members. However, it is important to structure their roles not as spies, but rather as positive reinforcers. The only type of data that you should allow a sibling to bring you is something that indicates your "target" has just earned a positive reinforcer. They can also be instructed to notice when he displays one of the pro-social behaviors and to reinforce him for it on the spot.

"Jane is trying to remember to wash her face when she comes to the table. It is really a hard thing to remember, so you can help her by

5. immediately   6. punishment   7. weak

telling her whenever you notice how clean her face is at breakfast or supper. When she forgets, don't say anything. No nagging, right?"

OBSERVING AND COUNTING

The social learning approach assumes that you are responsible for your own behavior, and that of the people in close contact with you. You can change your social environment; you can also make arrangements for changing your own behavior.

On the face of it, observing and counting just do not seem to be the kind of things you do when you wish to help someone. Behavior can, of course, be changed without anyone carrying out these activities. However, strange as it may seem at first, you are more likely to be successful if you take the additional time and care involved to observe and to count. Certainly, the improvements in your own behavior, or that of your child, are important enough--they are worth the additional five or ten minutes of your time required each day for these activities.

Observing and counting the behaviors may bring an interesting bonus, first noted by O. Lindsley.[6] The simple act of counting the occurrences of some of your own behaviors can serve to change their rate of occurrence! For example, if you wish to increase the time spent in reading, you might begin to count the number of minutes spent each day. For some, the act of observing and recording produces *increases* in reading. On the other hand, if you were interested in reducing "fingernail biting" or "angry thoughts about your spouse," daily recordings of these behaviors could produce decreases in their occurrence. In a sense, *careful* observation and record-keeping gives you better control over your own behavior.

61

Most of us do not observe either ourselves or anyone else very carefully. A curious fact pointed out by the Lindsley investigators is that *calmly* recording the incidence of a behavior occurring in the spouse or the child can serve to reduce the incidence of problem behaviors. Each time the child teases his sister, calmly state, "There is another one," as you record the event on a chart located on the refrigerator door. This is likely to produce a (8) _____ in rate. Such reductions may, of course be short-lived unless you also provide increased social reinforcers for the pro-social behavior that takes its place.

Aside from these "bonus" effects, another reason for collecting observation data lies in the fact that behavior usually changes slowly. If you have spent the required ten minutes a day observing and counting, then you can see that over time there has been a slow but perceptible decrease in the problem behavior. Without the data you might become discouraged and either give up altogether or shift your program. Some behavior changes may require *several weeks.* The daily sessions of collecting data serve as excellent reminders to carry out the rest of the program.

Get in the habit of collecting data on *anything* about your social environment that is of interest to you. Most professional behavior modifiers collect data on themselves and their loved ones. We do this, not because we "love science," but simply because it makes it possible to aid people we care about very much. Some also keep daily records on up to eight or ten of their own behaviors. Altogether such extensive record-keeping requires but a few minutes each day.

To be able to observe, you must first be able to "pinpoint" the behavior you are attempting to control. Pinpointing means *being specific.* What is it that you wish to change? "He is just

8. reduction

mean all the time" is *not* pinpointing the problem; the statement is much too vague. Specifically, what is it that he does that leads you to describe him as "mean"? As you watch him more carefully, you might note that he hits others, breaks their toys, says cruel things, and talks back to his parents. These are all countable. If you can't count the behavior, you have not pinpointed it properly.

Take the statement, "He is an immature child." How would you *count* that? Parents who complain about this usually go on to describe any one or all of the following: "He makes us do things for him that he can really do for himself (dress himself, feed himself), he talks baby talk, he whines, he cries all of the time, he will not play with other children but hangs onto his mother all day." The list of specific behaviors describing one immature child would not necessarily describe another. Each family must construct their own list.

In pinpointing your first problem, try to select one that occurs about five or more times a day. For example, teasing is a behavior which often fulfills this requirement. To pinpoint it for your child, first observe for a few days to see what it is that he does; write these behaviors down on a list. Tape the list to the refrigerator door where both of you can see it. You should also pinpoint its opposite. Specifically, what is it that you wish the child would do *instead of tease?* You might make a list of these behaviors, such as "play quietly with his brother," "sit and watch TV without fighting," "share things." You can set up two places on your daily data chart: one for "teases" and one for "pro-social." Once you agree on these specifics, then go to step two.

Step two involves the establishment of a baseline in which you observe and count behaviors for at least three or four days. Do not use a program at this time. Both parents should count the behaviors each day. If the behavior occurs more than once an hour, you can obtain a stable picture of what is going on by just observing for an hour or two each day.

The mother could observe during the morning and afternoon. The father could begin recording when he comes home from work and might continue until the child goes to bed. Each time the behaviors occur, make a mark on the data chart. If the response lasts more than one minute, you might mark it a second or third or fourth or fifth time if necessary. BOTH PARENTS OBSERVE.

Your baseline observations should cover at least three or four (9) d_____ . Compare notes and talk about what you are seeing. You should begin to get a much better understanding of this behavior. Particularly notice the reinforcers that keep it going. Most children will be curious about what this is all about. When asked, tell them; be brief and as non-punishing as possible.

"Mom, what is that junk on the refrigerator for, anyway? Are you counting me or what?" Mrs. J continued setting the table and said in a matter-of-fact voice, "Well, you know how much trouble you and Lari have with the teasing. Neither one of you seems to be able to stop it, so we thought we would try to help. Right now we are just counting each tease. Later we will do some things that will help you practice not teasing. I think if we all work together, we can change that and it will be better for everyone. By the way, once we start practicing the new thing, it should be fun for you and for Lari."

9. days

64

He may object to being counted and have a temper tantrum right on the spot. Ignore it. If you cannot ignore it, walk out of the room. Do not get involved in long debates with the child as to whether you have the right to observe and count his behavior. You *are* the parent and you *do* have the right. You may give the child a brief, *calm* description of what you are doing and why you are doing it. Do not (10) __de_____ .

It is helpful for recording either the high rate or low rate behaviors to wear a counter on your wrist. The most efficient piece of equipment seems to be a golfer's counter that can be bought for prices ranging from three to six dollars. Whether using a pencil and paper or a wrist counter, record your data *each* day on a data sheet. The chart which we have found useful looks like this; you can easily make your own.

DATA CHART

NAME *Scot*   OBSERVER *I*   DATE *2/11*

SPECIFIC BEHAVIORS PINPOINTED *"Swearing;" for example,*
says d-d, says s-, says s-o-b, and says b-.

DATE	FREQUENCY	TIME INTERVAL	MINUTES OR HOURS	RATE	COMMENTS
2/11 Mon	TTTT I	8:30am - 4pm	7½ hrs.	.8 per hr	
2/12 Tues	TTH TTH IIII	8:30am - 10pm	13½ hrs.	1.03	

Post this where everyone can find it. Each time an event occurs, label it, "That was a swear," record it, and *let it go*. No lectures, no

10. debate

nagging. At the end of the day add up the number of minutes or hours during which you observed and divide that into the number of behaviors you observed and put the resulting figure into the column labeled "rate." This makes it possible to compare a day when you only observed four hours to one on which you observed sixteen hours.

In summary, then, first pinpoint the behavior by drawing up a list of (11) _sp_____ behaviors that define the problem. Agree upon a time during which you will count. Record (12)_____ event on the data chart or wrist counter. When finished, record the time during which the observations were made. At the end of the day, calculate the rate by dividing the number of hours (or minutes) into the (13) _____ of times the behavior occurred. This gives you an estimate of (14) _r_____ . Keep this kind of data for three or four days.

You will find that there are ups and downs. The child may have a good day, and then several bad days. When you begin counting, he may have two or even three good days. If so, extend the baseline and continue counting to be sure that it is not just a honeymoon.

After you introduce programs to change the behavior, continue counting. Some programs go on for long periods of time; so it might be a good idea to graph the data so you can get a picture of what is happening. Just looking at a page of numbers can be very confusing. Putting the same material on graph paper helps to clarify basic trends in your program. Several blank sheets of graphing paper are included at the back of this book.

Let's suppose that the mean rate of swearing for a three-day baseline followed by a week's in-

11. specific   12. every, each
13. number   14. rate

tervention was: .80; 1.03; .98; 1.20; .80; .89; .70; .90; .60; .65. What do you make of all these numbers? Just by glancing at them it is difficult to tell what is going on. A graph can give you an overall picture at a glance. To prepare one, first label each column on the graph paper as a "day." That takes care of the bottom line. The rates for swearing for this boy went from a high point of 1.20, so that could be the top number for the vertical line. Set the bottom number at 0. Count each line between as .10. The first row is .00; the next is .10; the third row is .20; and so forth up to 1.20.

On the following graph, put in the numbers for the rows. The first day of the baseline was Monday, during which time Scot gave .80 swears per hour. On Tuesday, the second day, he gave 1.03 swears per hour; enter that on the graph. Now put in the data for the remaining days, given above. It helps in looking at the graph to connect the dots.

(15)   **GRAPH**

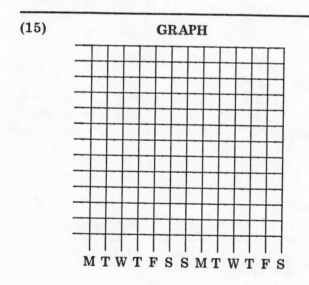

M T W T F S S M T W T F S

15. Answer on next page

In examining the data for this treatment program, it seems that there is a *very* gradual downward slope. He seems to be improving. Most of it, however, occurred on the last two days, which were (16) _____ and (17)_____ . While there is some progress, it does seem to be a weak program. I would continue the program for another two or three days; if the swearing didn't decrease further, then the program should be changed. Perhaps increasing the reinforcement for not swearing would help; we might also do something more effective to weaken swearing.

After your program has been underway for a few days you might encourage the child to begin recording when he believes the pro-social and/or problem behavior occurred. You might construct a chart for him on which he keeps his own data. At first, it might be wise to supervise him to be sure that you *both* agree on the behavior being counted. Reinforce him for correctly labeling and recording his own behavior. These procedures amount to the first steps in teaching a child to control his own behavior. Make very sure that what he says corresponds to what he does.

HOMEWORK

Part of your skill in assisting other people to change their behavior comes from your understanding how it works on yourself. Collect data on

15.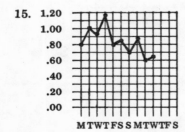

16. Tuesday

17. Wednesday

your *own behavior*. You will be more effective in your application of child management skills if you could, *today*, initiate a self-management program. You might count cigarettes, daily weight, yells, or arguments. Keep in mind that the programs do not *have* to involve changing undesirable behaviors. Why not pinpoint one of your behaviors that you wish to accelerate? For example, suppose you wish to increase the amount of time you spend on one of your hobbies, such as woodworking, or painting, or writing. Begin by counting the number of minutes each day that you spend *actually* engaging in that activity. Post a data chart or a graph in a prominent place, where you will notice it several times each day. Immediately after you have read, painted, or worked in the shop, post your time for that day on the chart.

Remember to keep your initial steps (18) _____. Do not try to put in several hours the first day. Put in fifteen or twenty minutes and stop when it becomes even slightly unpleasant. Again, your program for self-control will probably work best if you arrange *a specific time and place* for the activity. Have a room or a corner in the basement where you keep your materials and try to arrange things so that you can use them at the same time each day. Doing this plus keeping data will very likely give you some control over your behavior.

KEY IDEAS
A good program has many small steps.
Pinpoint the behaviors--BE SPECIFIC.
Observing is the first step in behavior control.
A baseline is at least three days.
Also keep data during intervention.
Observe and graph your own behavior.
You make your own social environment.

18. small

eight

Contracts

"Contracts" is an odd, almost unfriendly term to use when discussing better ways of getting along with other people. However, we have found it indispensable in assisting adults in getting along better with each other. As used here, it means writing down the specific behaviors and the reinforcing arrangements that are agreed upon by the two or more persons involved. Writing such an agreement is a means of being specific and it is also a commitment. As a document, it is likely to be brought out many times to solve disputes about what someone *really* said in the original agreement.

Just as a rule of thumb, the older the persons involved, the more important it is that the agreement be negotiated by both parties. In attempting to work out behavior change agreements with adolescents or spouses, negotiation is mandatory. There are several investigators who have written technical reports describing the use of such contracts; the papers by L. Homme,[4] R. Stuart,[27] and E. Phillips[22] would be most worthwhile.

It seems to be easiest to negotiate with the younger child because generally these contracts only involve a single problem. The parents specify the problem behaviors and the pro-social behaviors which will replace them. After explaining the idea of the program and earning points to the child, ask him to select the back-up reinforcer.

"Okay, Jim, each time you come right home after school, you earn points. If you are home at 4:00, you get three points. At 4:30 you get two points, and at 5:00, you get one point. Any later than that, and you have to do dishes that night.

"You could earn fifteen points this week. What would you like to earn for ten points?" Jim still acts as if he is being scolded (the usual thing in his house) and stands staring at the floor. His mother comments, "When you earn fifteen points, you could take the whole family to the pizza parlor, and you decide what we order." Jim looks more interested as his father suggests, "How about ten points means you and I go fishing Sunday afternoon on the McKenzie?" Jim finally says, "Could I get a new hot wheels set?" The mother waits for another suggestion and when none is forthcoming, "Well, no, that is a little too expensive. How about for this first week just earning a new car for the set you have? Maybe later on we could talk about a whole new set. Is there anything else you would like to work for?" "No, the car is okay."

Following the discussion, the agreement and point chart are taped to the refrigerator door.

"COMING HOME PROGRAM" JIM SEPT. 15

M	T	W	T	F	M	T	W	T	F	M	T	W	T	F	M	T	W	T
3	2	0	3	3	3													

Jim gets three points for being home at 4:00.
       two   points   4:30.
       one   point   5:00.

He does dishes that night if he comes in after 5:30.

When he earns 10 points, he gets to pick out a new car for his hot wheels set.

_____   _____   _____

Jim   Mom   Dad

As noted earlier, for a successful program it is necessary to use (1) s͟o͟c͟i͟a͟l͟ reinforcers as well as the points. Mention each day how well he is doing; brag about his improvements to your friends.

For the first agreement, keep the step small. He should earn his first back-up reinforcer in a week or less. If he is a young child, the time interval might be only a day or two. Do not pay off for "almost performance"; see that he really earns what he gets but try to set the initial step so that he is almost certain to earn his back-up reinforcer.

After he has earned his first back-up reinforcer, he may select a different one for the next step. Give him suggestions if he needs them, but try to respond to what it is that *he wants to do*. It need not involve buying him things. Sometimes children more enjoy working for things just because they would be "fun." For example, they get to sit in the father's chair at supper, or they get to decide what desserts the family eats for a week. Most children seem to particularly enjoy earning their parents' time. "Getting mother" for a morning in the park, or father for an afternoon at a

1. social

movie theater are apparently powerful reinforcers for many children.

There is a somewhat more complex contract that is useful with the older child (six through adolescence). It is introduced only after the child has been involved in one or two prior programs so that he has some general idea of the format. First, construct a list of problems that occur each day. These are generally things that the child neglects to do. They are presented to the child in such a way that he earns points for "doing the right thing." The list particularly emphasizes the positive things that you wish him to do rather than being a list of "sins." For example:

DANA'S PROGRAM									
	M	T	W	T	F	S	S	M	T
BRUSH TEETH	✓	✓							
MAKE BED	✓								
CLEAN UP ROOM	✓	✓							
GREET PEOPLE		✓							
GET TO SCHOOL ON TIME	✓	✓							
DO HOMEWORK		✓							
HELP WITH DISHES	✓	✓							
TOTAL 5 6									

Dana gets one point for each behavior. When she gets 25 points, she can have Cynthia come and stay overnight.

It is a good idea to record the points immediately after the behavior occurs. When you give the child a mark, accompany it with a (2) s_____ re_____. Do not give lectures about the behaviors which did not occur.

2. social reinforcer

73

Simply indicate that, "You forgot to brush your teeth, so no points for that."

The advantage of using this checklist, of course, is that you can simultaneously strengthen a whole set of behaviors that occur *sometimes*, but are still relatively weak and unpredictable. It saves you the necessity of carrying out a series of six or seven programs.

The idea of the checklist can be extended to cover situations where you are not present, for example, at school, time spent with the baby sitter, or weekends with the grandparents. In this situation the contract must, of course, be negotiated with the child and with the adults who are immediately present in the situations, such as the teacher, the baby sitter, or the grandparents. Typically they will have some idea from previous experience with the child as to the kind of problems they encounter and which pro-social behaviors need to be strengthened.

The checklist on the next page was constructed for a child who displayed a wide range of out-of-control behaviors. The contract stipulated that the *parents* provide consequences for behaviors that occur in school. The mother called the teacher each day in order to get the specific information. This type of concerted teamwork brought the behaviors under control in relatively short order. The child's world suddenly became quite predictable in terms of providing "payoffs" for adaptive child behaviors; it also provided for mild but fair punishment for problem behaviors. The child is always aware of what is on the checklist. He helps set the "price" for each item, sees the results each day, and negotiates the back-up reinforcers for the points. The contract is changed from time to time, as are the (3)_____ - _____ reinforcers.

3. back-up

DAVE'S PROGRAM	M	T	W	T	F	S
GETS TO SCHOOL ON TIME (2)	2					
DOES NOT ROAM AROUND ROOM (1)	0					
DOES WHAT THE TEACHER TELLS HIM (5)	3					
GETS ALONG WELL WITH OTHER KIDS (5)	1					
COMPLETES HIS HOMEWORK (5)	2					
WORK IS ACCURATE (5)	3					
BEHAVIOR ON THE SCHOOLBUS IS OK (2)	2					
GETS ALONG WELL WITH BROTHER AND SISTERS IN EVENING (3)	0					

TOTAL   13

1. If Dave gets 25 points, he doesn't have to do any chores that night, and he gets to pick all the TV shows for the family to watch.
2. If Dave gets only 15 points, he does not get to watch TV that night.
3. If Dave gets only 10 points, he gets no TV and he also has to do the dishes.
4. If Dave gets only 5 points or less, then no TV, wash dishes, and is grounded for the next two days (home from school at 4:00 and stay in yard).

When working with several settings like this, you should be prepared for repeated changes in the contract in order to get one that really fits. If you are strengthening a large number of behaviors, you should also plan on continuing the use of the contracts for several weeks or months.

Graphing the weekly point totals will help you know where you are. When you believe the behaviors are under control, you might begin collecting data every other day. If things continue to look good, try collecting data only once a week. The child's behavior will tell you if you are moving too fast. If your steps are too large, then you will lose control of the (4) be_____. If

4. behavior

this happens, just go back and make the steps (5)_____, increase the value of the (6) b_____ - _____ r_____, or use more social reinforcement.

Just as was the case for collecting data, writing down agreements can become a "habit" and is probably a good one to acquire. For example, the simple matter of recording on the wall calendar the initials of the children who "did dishes" requires little time, but saves much debating such as, "I did them two weeks ago!" "No, I did!"

Similarly, recording such simple agreements as the following can save many arguments.

Craig can use the car, when it is available on week nights, but must be in by 10:30. On weekends he can keep it out until 12:30 on one night. He pays for all the gas for any trips out of town. He pays for the insurance. In case of accidents, he pays for repairs. If he gets in later than the agreement, he loses the car for one week for each hour that he is late.

This agreement was arrived at only after a good deal of discussion with Craig. It was also changed several times as new problems came up and were discussed. The agreement was not "handed down" by the parents, but rather represents a series of compromises that only partially pleased either Craig or his parents. Each side had to give a little in order to produce the contract.

As a general principle, it is probably a good idea to write down any agreements among adults (adolescents) that concern time, work, or money.

5. smaller   6. back-up reinforcer

KEY IDEAS
Negotiate contracts with children.
Be specific.
Write it down.

nine

Time Out

The term "Time Out" (TO) means time out from reinforcement. The young child is removed from a situation that is reinforcing problem behavior to one that is not at all reinforcing. This arrangement has proven to be a most effective means of producing *rapid* decreases in the occurrence of problem behaviors. It is also something that can replace spanking, which is the kind of punishment most parents use.

If you ignore undesirable behavior, it will be weakened. Given enough time, such an arrangement is very likely to work, but in the meantime, the long-suffering parent or teacher has to put up with several hundred temper tantrums, teases, hits, or whines. **TO** is an extension of the idea of non-reinforcement, but extended in a way which makes it much more effective in bringing about *rapid* changes in behavior.

The child is removed from the situation where all of the reinforcers are and he is placed in a new situation where there are few, if any. For example, if he teases, he might be placed in the bathroom for five minutes; this is a dull, non-reinforcing place. He is placed there *every* time he teases. The effect of a number of pairings of teasing and **TO** will be that the behavior is

78

(1) w_____ . Generally the effect is noticeable within three to four days.

Most parents have been trained by children to rely upon the twin parental crutches, "scold" and "spank." As described in an earlier section, these parent behaviors will usually turn off the aversive behavior for a short time. This short-term reduction in "pain" (2) r_____ the parents for scolding and spanking. Unfortunately, spanking often produces an emotional aftermath that is unpleasant for both the parent and child. As most parents are reluctant to get involved in such an emotional scene very often, they spank only every tenth or hundredth time the problem behaviors occur. When they spank often depends upon how they happen to feel at the moment. What this means, of course, is that between spankings the child receives all kinds of reinforcement from his siblings. While periodically he may get spanked, adding up the amount of strengthening and weakening involved would show that the behavior is only affected on a short-term basis and may actually show long-term increases in rate.

Parents who are willing to track very carefully and punish each time are effective but then they must pay the emotional price tag attached to this approach. There may be an emotional price tag attached to the first few times TO is used. TO is a mild punishment but it is an effective substitute for hitting, spanking, yelling, and lecturing. It can be used a dozen times a day at little cost to the parent. Rather than waiting until the child's behavior is so obnoxious that you are upset and angry, TO can be introduced early in the behavioral chain. It is used when the children are just beginning to get wound up and before the teasing and fighting begin.

In using TO you would begin by pinpointing and counting both the problem behavior and the

1. weakened   2. reinforces

pro-social behavior that will take its place. It is generally a good idea to first begin the reinforcement point program involved in strengthening the pro-social behavior so that the overall amount of reinforcement for the child is increased. The general effect is to make it indirectly reinforcing for the child to participate in the program. In other words, before applying non-reinforcement and **TO** you must be sure the child is receiving adequate (3) _____ for *some* behaviors. If you tend to use very few social reinforcers in interacting with your child, make doubly sure that you have a reinforcement program underway before using non-reinforcement or **TO**. Reinforcement and shaping procedures should be the solid foundations upon which you build child management procedures, with the main emphasis upon positive reinforcement, shaping pro-social behaviors, and using contracts and point programs.

TO is most effective for high rate behaviors found in younger children between the ages of two and twelve. For older children, it might be necessary to negotiate some other type of aversive consequences for certain behaviors. For example, coming in late in the evening would not earn **TO** but would mean "grounded for a week." Swearing would lead to neither **TO** nor a lecture, but rather to the calm statement, "That word cost you 25¢." These consequences must be established *in advance* and preferably written down.

The first consideration in using **TO** lies in the selection of a place. It should have several characteristics, but primarily it should be *very dull*. It should symbolize all that is non-reinforcing. That means no toys, no TV, no books, *no people*. In the home, the bathroom is the most likely spot. For the child who is extremely active or destructive, it might be necessary to remove all of the objects from the medi-

3. reinforcement

cine cabinet. If, as is frequently the case, the child runs water all over the floor, he earns a natural consequence of cleaning it up (after his TO is completed). Give no lectures; simply state, "You must clean up the bathroom floor before you watch TV tonight." Clearly state what the (4) c_____ will be for noncompliance to the request. Be specific about what you mean by "clean up the mess," and spell out the consequence for not "cleaning up the mess."

For the classroom a screen in one corner of the room with a chair placed behind it is adequate for TO for most unmanageable children. Make sure that the child is not readily visible to the other children. Extremely unmanageable children may have to serve TO in the nurse's office for a day or two before the screen-chair ensemble is effective.

Parents often have strong feelings about putting their child into the bathroom and make a case for putting a chair in the hallway or sitting in the corner as alternatives. However, this usually does not work, because there are *people* in these areas and people are just naturally "reinforcing." One of the first requirements for proper use of TO is that is must be in a (5)_____ place. If you observe the amount of social interaction that occurs around a child sitting in a corner of the kitchen, you can easily ascertain that it is not "non-reinforcing." In fact, he may get more reinforcement there than at most other times in his day. But collect data and see. If your data show that standing in the corner for five minutes is decelerating the behavior you want to change, then it "works" for your child. Three days of consistent use of TO should reduce the rates of most problem behaviors.

Again, many parents say, "But I've used that for years and it didn't work. I send him to his room all the time and it never works." Closer

4. consequence(s)   5. non-reinforcing, dull

checking reveals the parent did *not* send him to the bedroom *every time*. In fact, the room had a full complement of toys, comic books, and TV. By definition, this is *not* TO. TO must be used consistently and carried out in a place that is essentially (6) _____ .

TO differs in several respects from the normal expedient of sending the child to his room: (1) Most parents do *not* send the child to his room *every* time; (2) Most children's bedrooms are full of reinforcing things; and (3) TO is used for only a short period of time (three to five minutes), while "being sent to your room" could mean a sentence ranging from thirty minutes to all day. These long sentences are for the parents' benefit; they feel better having the child out of their hair. TO, on the other hand, keeps the child out of the parents' way for only three to five minutes and the parents must work hard to keep track of the time so the child does *not* spend long periods of time in isolation. Research with children has shown that one to five minutes of TO are as effective as twenty to thirty minutes of TO.[21] Actually, it is wise to set a kitchen timer when the child goes into TO so that the end of the time interval is clearly signaled for both parent and child.

Putting a child into TO requires some artistry. The arrangement should be specified beforehand so that you do not find yourself attempting to "explain" its use when both you and the child are very angry.

"I know you have trouble remembering not to interrupt people when they are talking. I also know that you are tired of having your mother and me nag you about it all of the time. We have a program that

6. non-reinforcing, dull

will help you practice not interrupting people. I think it might even be fun for you.

"First, if you can go all evening without interrupting anyone, you get five points. Each time you interrupt, you lose one point. We will keep track each day. When you get twenty points, that is worth three comic books; or is there something else you would like to earn?

"To help with the practice we are also going to use **TO**. Each time you interrupt someone, we will tell you and then you go into **TO**. We will set the timer so that it rings at the end of five minutes. You go into the bathroom and wait for it to go off; then you come out."

Some parents arrange for any family member who interrupts to go into Time Out. This seems a fair arrangement. When the actual occasion for **TO** arrives, *be calm. Do not* (7) _sc_____ or (8) _na_____ .

"Whoops, you did it. That was an interruption. Five minutes in **TO**; I will set the timer so that you know when to come out."

Do not debate the legality of the situation; be very firm. If he insists on debating, inform him that each minute of debate means another minute in (9) _____ . Ignore his arguments other than to inform him "one minute more," "two minutes more," and so forth. When he has earned thirty to forty minutes of time,

7. scold   8. nag   9. Time Out

you might inform him that if he does not go into **TO** within the next minute, he will lose TV rights for that night (or lose dessert, the bicycle, or the right to leave the yard). *Be certain* that this back-up consequence is followed through on that *very night*. If you forget to back up your statements, then you have really lost the interchange and things will be worse the next time. Do not physically drag him into **TO**; calmly state what the consequence for his noncompliance is and then walk away.

Some children, really well trained in manipulating adults, may say something like, "Go ahead, put me in the bathroom; I like it in there." Using this Br'er Rabbit in the briar patch routine, many children can actually talk their parents out of using **TO**. Go ahead and use **TO**, collect data on the behavior you are decelerating, and see what three days of *consistent* application of **TO** does. His words may or may not tell you what will work. YOUR DATA TELL YOU WHAT WORKS.

Many children will attempt to come out of the **TO** room, talk to people, yell, cry, or kick the door. If they break anything in the room during **TO**, then naturally they must pay for it out of their allowance. For each kick, yell, or attempt to peek out of the **TO** room, add one more minute of **TO**. Tell him when he gets out that each response costs him more time. Each minute of yelling or crying would elicit the same response. If he comes out before time is up and refuses to re-enter, state your back-up consequence and *then ignore him.* "Unless you go to **TO** immediately, your bike will be locked up; it will stay locked up for two days." Do not become engaged in arguments, debates, or lectures about whether you have the right to do this.

If the child was originally sent into **TO** for a failure to comply with some request, repeat the request when he comes out of **TO**. If he noncomplies again, return him to (10)_____ . When

10. Time Out

84

he has completed that round, repeat the
(11) _____ .

If the children act up in the car or at the
store, they can be told that they are earning TO;
this assumes, of course, that the procedure has
previously been in effect in the home. The child is
placed in TO as soon as you arrive home.

Kurt was a nine-year-old boy living in a
comfortable home. He kept the family continually off-balance with high rates of teasing his
younger sister, humiliating his mother, and non-
complying to requests made by either parent. The
parents often engaged in bitter arguments about
whose fault it was. They tried all of the usual
nostrums to correct his behavior and their own.
Spankings and severe punishments had no effect,
nor did bribes. He was placed on a point system
in which he earned points for each hour during
which one of the behaviors did not occur and TO
for each occurrence of the behavior. Figure 1
shows what happened to "noncompliance,"
"humiliation," and "teasing."

FIGURE 1

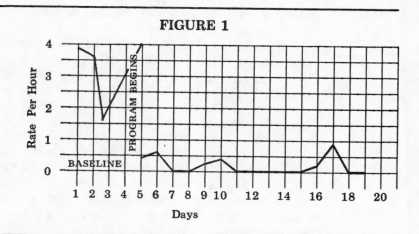

11. request

During baseline Kurt was inflicting three or four of these behaviors on members of his family *every hour!* By the end of the first day of the program he was displaying only one of these behaviors every two or three hours. Results are not usually this dramatic. For many families, the first day may actually show an *increase* in rate of problem behaviors.

Notice that even though Kurt had been on the program for several days, there was one point where the rate of problem behavior again climbed to .2 and then .65 per hour. This happened on day (12)_____ and day (13)_____ . On these "bad days" the parents simply used **TO** and again brought the problems under control. At the end of two weeks this was a much different home; a much happier one for everyone concerned, including Kurt. Even when the behavior is reasonably under control, use **TO** whenever the problems recur in the future. Behavior does *not* just disappear; rather, it will tend to recur from time to time. When this happens, your reactions will determine whether the problem behaviors are strengthened or weakened. You do construct your own social world, but it is also up to you to keep it in repair.

When using **TO** be certain that you remain calm. In addition, be sure to apply it each (14)_____ the problem behavior occurs. *Both* parents participate in using the point program and **TO**. It is often the case that the father is particularly reluctant to use either one.

Often, there are regular chains of events which lead up to the problem behavior. **TO** should be used to interrupt these chains. For example, hitting is usually the outcome of a prolonged argument or a teasing interchange. If this is the case, use **TO** to weaken the earlier members of this chain such as "arguing" or "teasing."

12. ten   13. seventeen   14. time, occasion

It has probably occurred to you that there are really many variations on the TO theme. They have been developed individually by persons attempting to live together. For example, some parents have simply removed themselves from the home for a half-hour or longer when the children's behavior gets too obnoxious. Married couples also report the use of "stony silence" which may last for hours or days as a kind of prolonged TO for behaviors which are disapproved of. In all of these instances, the individual is deciding that he will no longer provide reinforcement for the person whose behavior he is attempting to alter. TO, then, is a natural consequence already in use by many persons.

KEY IDEAS

TO is a mild, but effective, punishment.

TO means time out from reinforcement.

Physical punishment is generally followed by emotional disturbances.

When using TO, be certain to *also* increase the use of positive reinforcement for some pro-social behavior.

One to five minutes of TO is sufficient.

Be consistent.

Keep data.

Both parents should use TO.

Section Three

Applications to Ordinary Family Problems

This section details the application of the procedures for handling problems that come up in almost all families. Because general child management problems have served as the focus for much of the discussion thus far, it was thought expedient to set aside a special section for "adult management." The problem of how one goes about altering the behavior of one's wife or husband can, of course, become a central problem for a family. While the procedures of pinpointing, data collection, and social reinforcement have some general utility for such problems, they may prove less effective than they do for child management problems.

The material in this section was developed as part of a two-year research project on married couples in various degrees of marital conflict. The studies are described in a series of research reports.[15] As we get more experience, the present procedures will be extended and revised. Future revisions of this volume will reflect these changes.

ten

Exchange

Thus far we have concentrated upon the skills required for the adult learning to deal with younger children. While important, these skills will probably not handle problems that come up among older members of the family. The general ideas of the reinforcement of desirable behavior and non-reinforcement for undesirable behavior *might* produce slow changes over long periods of time. However, each of the adults in the family is being reinforced for many things by people who are not in the immediate family. The father, for example, is reinforced not only by family members, but also by colleagues at work and on the golf course. His peers may be reinforcing him for the very things that the family members are attempting to weaken. The wife and the adolescent child also have many contacts with close friends outside the family who have significant effects in controlling their behavior. Taken together, these considerations lead us to assume that the older the individual, the more difficult it is to change his behavior. The reason for the difficulty lies in the fact that with increasing age, it becomes more difficult to retrain all of the people who (1) _____ him for his usual mode of doing things.

1. reinforce

It is necessary, therefore, to follow somewhat different procedures in programming changes for older members of the family. While we will continue to use social reinforcers, pinpointing, and keeping data, it will be necessary to explore some additional means of negotiating changes in each other's behavior. The additional procedures are analogous to ancient ideas about "bartering" and to modern sociological exchange theory. Those persons who wish to explore this in more detail are urged to study W. J. Lederer and D. D. Jackson's *The Mirages of Marriage*, 1968.[5]

In order to live together in a closed group, it is *necessary to change each other's behavior*. If individuals get into conflict at work, there are rules and procedures for arbitrating such changes. If these procedures don't work, you can generally avoid these unpleasant people. If all else fails, you may decide to leave. The rules, arbitration procedures, and relative freedom to avoid or leave usually keep conflict within manageable limits. In the home, however, these *safety valves are not operative*. There are seldom clear-cut rules for arbitration and it is almost impossible to leave.

To make the problem more difficult, people within the family are constantly *changing over time*. This is particularly true of the adolescent who is being trained by his peers. Each change requires other family members to adjust by somehow changing too. For example, when the adolescent learns to drive the family car, this will have an effect on other family members.

Requests for behavior change are a *normal* part of living together as a family. Interestingly enough, they usually are concerned with "little things." How does a wife go about getting her husband to pick up his clothes that he leaves lying about every day? This is a *small thing*. On the other hand, he does it every day. If one after another of these small things pile up and do not change, their accumulative effect is to produce large-scale conflicts. These "little things" can lead to changes in the way we feel about each other.

Conflicts arise when one person DEMANDS IMMEDIATE CHANGES in the behavior of another person and the other person noncomplies. These demands are often accompanied by aversive statements. One person demands immediate change; the other refuses. This defines (2) _conflict_. For example, the statement, "Shut up, you idiot," is a demand for immediate behavior (3)_change_ . It also contains the negative evaluation term "idiot," which is (4) _aversive_ to the other person. The use of aversive words makes it likely that the other person will counterattack rather than comply. In this situation, behavior will *not* change.

By this definition it takes (5) _two_ people to have a conflict--one who demands immediate changes in behavior and one who refuses to comply. If the interchange has occurred many times in the past, and no changes in behavior followed, then the exchanges are more likely to be accompanied by aversive statements by both persons.

"Please pick up your clothes. Everyday I have to go around and pick up after you. I'm not your mother. You act just like a little boy." He hardly looks up from reading the paper, "Listen, I work ten hours a day, six days a week. When I come home I want peace and quiet and I sure as hell don't want to be nagged. You are just like your mother—everything has to be perfect. Nag, nag, all of the time!" At this point her voice raises and she shouts, "I'm not a slave in this house, either!"....and he responds....she responds, etc.

2. conflict   3. change   4. aversive   5. two

She is demanding behavior change *and* punishing at the same time. When she does this, the spouse is likely to respond in kind. When this happens, you have two people (6) _____ each other, but no behavior changes. After hundreds of these interchanges, one or both members are likely to stop listening or perhaps even stop interacting. Punishing the other person by insulting him, yelling at him, or nagging him about past wrongs will only lead to a situation where the other person either avoids you or attacks you in turn. In any case, both of you will be sidetracked.

You may try a hundred times, but each time the dialogue gets sidetracked. Instead of designing a behavior change program, you end up hurting each other. In this context, then, when discussing a program for behavior change, the use of (7) p_____ leads to (8) side_____ .

After many months of unsuccessful effort there are so many different problems accumulated that no time or place in the household is free from strife.

As the first step, pick a discussion *time* and *place.* Select a quiet room and select only the two or three persons directly involved. Agree upon a negotiating *time.* Literally make an *appointment.* At first, the sessions should be relatively brief, for example, ten to twenty minutes. It is probably best to keep half an hour as the upper limit. Work on only *one* problem per session. If a particular problem is pressing, it might be wise to provide for regular daily sessions. In advanced stages of conflict, the mere presence of the person in the room becomes a stimulus for hassling; going in the car together to a party can set the occasion for bitter strife. If this is the case for you, do *not* negotiate at other times during the day. If a problem comes up, say, "Well, O.K. That sounds important, but let's wait until our discussion time at 4:00 today." If both

6. punishing, hurting   7. punishment
8. sidetracking

members do this, they will teach other to stop the continuous, mutual harassment.

Assuming that you have selected a regular (9) _____ and (10) _____ for your negotiations, there are rules of procedure to follow. Each should come to the discussion "armed" only with paper and pencil. One person serves as secretary and keeps a regular logbook. Everyone observes and labels aversive comments. These would include attempts to go over past histories of wrongs and grievances, insulting statements, attempts to blame the other person for the present difficulties and threats. If you are well-practiced combatants, you will be amazed at how much of your interaction is characterized by these behaviors. When one occurs, the offended member must label it, "That was a zap (punishment)," and it is recorded in the logbook. Agree in advance how many such occurrences are tolerable, i.e., two, three, four. When the agreed upon number occurs, the meeting is terminated for *that day*. You may find that many of your first meetings are interrupted early. You might decide to use monetary fines so that each zap costs the person a quarter. The victim is *always* the one to decide if he has just been punished. He knows when he has been hurt. Don't let the punisher talk you out of it by, "Oh, was that a zap? No one would call *that* a zap!" If the victim says it hurts, it *is* a zap.

The successful design of behavior change programs presupposes that you first teach each other to stop punishing when discussing behavior change programs. Step two requires that you are able to discuss conflicts with "zero zapping."

When negotiating, *take turns* so that each person has *equal* time. Do not use your time going over ancient histories of hurts and wrongs. Stay in the present and pinpoint changes in the behavior of the other person that would make

9. time   10. place

94

your life more pleasant. Talk only about the
(11) pr_____ and be (12) sp_____ .
List the specific behaviors of the other person
that you would like to have changed. Take five
or ten minutes to pinpoint one problem behavior.
During that time the other person just *listens.* No
arguments or debates while the speaker specifies
what the behaviors are that hurt him. During the
pinpointing, the speaker must also specify one
positive behavior displayed by the other person
that makes him feel good. Stay in the
(13) _____ , be specific, and pinpoint
both a positive and an aversive behavior in each
session. Only (14)_____ problem per session.

Pinpointing simply means that you be
(15) sp_____ . List which behaviors of the
other person please you *and* which you wish to
have (16) _____ . For example, "I wish
my wife were a better housekeeper," is *not* pinpointing behavior. A pinpoint must be so clear
that the behavior can be *observed* and *counted.*
The listener might help at this point by asking,
"What does 'better housekeeper' mean?"

"Well, you know, I'd like to
have the living room picked up when
I come home." His wife sits writing
down the statement, looking a bit
angry, but says nothing. "I'd like to
have you put your stuff away that
you leave in the bathroom." At this
point she slams down the notebook
on the floor and retorts, "Some of
that is your junk, too, and the kids',
so what about that?" "Okay, Zelda,
that was a zap. You attacked me and
didn't let me finish. Save it for your

11. present   12. specific   13. present   14. one
15. specific   16. changed

turn. I'd like to have the dishes washed and put away, too. Okay? I like the way you bring me coffee at night when I'm reading."

The behaviors which he listed were specific and there was little argument about whether or not the behavior had occurred. The wife made a similar list of specific messy behaviors displayed by her husband, including such things as his throwing clothes on the closet floor, leaving newspapers strewn around the floor, and storing junk in the garage. It may require several discussion sessions to pinpoint. You have plenty of time; keep your negotiations short and calm. If you don't solve a problem, come back to it later.

Once the lists are written down, you are ready for the next step: EXCHANGE PIN-POINTED ITEMS. Beginning with item one on her husband's list, Zelda agreed that she would change her behavior vis-a-vis her articles left lying about the living room. However, he in turn must pick up the newspapers he throws on the floor each evening. She also agreed that the dishes would be washed and stored away if he would neatly box and store his "collection" in the garage. When the list of specific behaviors is available, it is surprising how well the exchange can be negotiated.

RECORD ALL LISTS AND EXCHANGES. Items and agreements are easily forgotten by even the best-intentioned people. Protect yourselves from future disagreements, "I said...," "No, you really said...," by the simple expedient of writing them down. These contracts are too important to leave to the tender mercies of fallible memory.

Before you can trade behaviors to be changed, the problem behaviors must first be (17) p_____ . Then (18)_____

17. pinpointed   18. write

96

them down. Good intentions and writing things down don't necessarily produce behavior change. Most persons experience a brief "honeymoon" period after making a contract. However, eventually, as in the case of New Year's resolutions, they slip back into old ways and the problem behaviors may reappear. For this reason, the last step in negotiating may be crucial, for it makes provisions for consequences. These consequences reduce the likelihood of slipping back to old ways. Each person should stipulate what the consequence will be for *his* violating the agreement. Zelda and her husband agreed that any articles of clothing left lying about would be deposited in a "Saturday Box." This contribution by O. Lindsley requires that deposits remain in the box until Saturday, at which time they are returned to their owners. Monetary fines might also be leveled; the amounts should be agreed upon in advance and written into the contract.

Each of us is continually changing. It is likely that two or more people who live together will have a continuing need to negotiate the changes in each other's behaviors. A change in one family member may pose problems for the other members, and negotiation and renegotiation may be necessary. Once a contract has been set up, it is often necessary to renegotiate parts, or all, of the contract. In this context it might be interesting to contemplate agreements with spouses to *accelerate* behaviors which both agree would be desirable. One spouse might, for example, trade an hour of reading for her spouse's taking a relaxing walk. Why not negotiate "growth" or "self-improving" behaviors?

SOME PRACTICAL APPLICATIONS

Bill and Betty were young, attractive people. They were socially skilled and both moderately successful in their fields. She managed a small boutique and he ran a small business from an office in their home. Their two children were both in school, but in the past year had been showing increasing rates of out-of-control behavior at home and in school. While the parents were able to learn how to handle the children's problems by participating as members of the parent training program, they returned some months later to describe a marriage which had been steadily deteriorating for the past few years.

They found that most of their time spent together served as a setting for endless bickering and increasingly intense conflicts. Within the past month the husband had mentioned the possibility of divorce. Much of their conflicts centered around "her working" and "her coldness" and "his nagging" and "his worrying about money." They received a series of half a dozen training sessions in which they were trained to pinpoint problems without sidetracking, negotiate exchanges and consequences, and write contracts. The details of these procedures and the data showing the changes in behaviors are presented in a report published elsewhere.[15]

They wrote a series of contracts which laid the groundwork for profound changes in both their own and the behavior of their children. The first contract required several weeks of effort. It was particularly difficult for the husband to pinpoint what it was about his wife's behavior that bothered him, and what it was that was a reinforcer. For example, he began by saying that, "She is nice to be around." After some searching, it turned out that he really liked it when she would sit and talk to him about his work and the family. Her sitting and talking about her own work, or sitting and fixing her nails was not a "Please." She, on the other hand, could be quite specific in saying that she appreciated his getting supper ready when she came in late from work.

The following contract was their first effort and was constructed under close supervision.

Changes that Betty wants to see in Bill:

1. Discuss money *once* a week for about 15 minutes or less.
2. Nag only once a month.
3. No nagging about her job unless the routine is changed.
4. If he slips up and does more nagging than this, the consequence will be to buy her a dress on the household account ($20.00).

Changes that Bill wants to see in Betty:

1. Deviations from the present work routine are upsetting. The present routine includes: M, 9-5:30; Tu, 5-9; W, off; Th, 5-9; F, 9-1; no Sat. or Sun. If the routine is broken (Betty comes home late or works on a weekend), this costs Betty $5.00 from her checking account.
2. When Bill can afford to give Betty $100 per month for herself, then she quits work.

_____   _____
Betty   Bill

For a few days things were wonderful. Bill did not nag and Betty managed to stay with her work schedule. However, in the next week there was sufficient backsliding to cost both of them a substantial amount of money. When the first "nag" occurred, Betty felt that the whole thing was rather hopeless and that Bill could not change. She also said that the $20.00 just was not that important to her and maybe she should just let it go by. However, she was encouraged to "collect" her just reward and to believe that *over time* Bill would change.

Behavior Does not Change Overnight.
It is not Words,
but Consequences that Change Behavior.

Both Bill and Betty collected consequences for the next week and gradually the behaviors in their first contract were brought under control. At this point they were encouraged to try some further negotiations for other problems. After their experience with the first contract, they were able to pinpoint the problems much more clearly as is evidenced in the following contract.

AGREEMENT #2

Pinpoints for Bill:

1. Bill hangs his clothes on bedposts and throws them on the bureau. He shall pay $5.00 for each article of clothing placed on the above-named particulars.
2. Bill throws newspapers about the floor when finished reading. If he violates the above, he shall mop the floor and/or wash the windows for not less than three (3) days.
3. Bill does not and will not replace shaving materials after using. If Bill violates the above, Betty can put such materials into a hiding place for not more than three (3) days.

Pinpoints for Betty:

1. Betty does not place her shoes on her shoe rack when coming home from work. Betty shall pay the amount of $5.00 for each pair of shoes not placed on the proper shoe rack.
2. Betty leaves dinner dishes overnight. Betty, violating the above, shall wash the Volkswagen and clean the interior.
3. Betty does not keep her bathroom neat from cosmetics, etc. If she violates the above, Bill can put such articles into a hiding place for not more than three (3) days.

_____   _____
Betty   Bill

As the rate of conflicts dropped, they began discussing more general aspects of their marriage and family life. Each relationship has some implied agreements which really must be specified and pinpointed. From their discussions they discovered the importance of each of them living a separate life as well as a life as a member of the family. Bill, for example, had given up all of his former interests and friends. Betty, on the other hand, had become so immersed in her work that she was but little involved as a member of the family. The following pinpointing of general agreements and exchanges was worked out entirely by Bill and Betty.

Spending more time alone--Bill will play golf and Betty will get baby sitter and do her thing alone (spend some time with her friends). This shall occur not more than once a week. If one party chooses not to do his thing, this is all right. But if the other party chooses to do his or her thing, he or she may. If Bill chooses to do something other than golf, he may do whatever he wishes. This shall be strictly during the daytime.

Spending more time together by taking weekend trips not less than three times a year. Betty shall see that proper arrangements are made for the children. A time shall be set for this and if one party refuses to go at this time, the consequences will be that the dissenting party will have to sacrifice his or her time alone (as in paragraph I). It is all right if both parties agree not to go at the planned time.

Bill has permitted Betty to work more hours, provided she does not work more than two nights a week and no weekends, or perhaps one-half day on Saturdays. This has to follow a stable schedule during the week. The consequences are $5.00 for every time she works an irregular schedule. If Bill harasses Betty during a normal routine in schedule, then he owes her $5.00.

_____   _____
Betty   Bill

As described in the published report, there were satisfying reductions in rates of conflicts within the home. They spent more time talking with each other and more time together as a family. At the time of this writing, there has been no divorce. Most importantly, both felt that they had produced changes in their own behavior and felt they could handle like problems in the future.

KEY IDEAS

Conflict is a demand for immediate change followed by a noncompliance.

Aversive statements produce aversive statements.

Aversive statements lead to sidetracking.

Choose a regular time and place for negotiation.

Stay in the present.

Pinpoint behavior changes and behaviors which "please."

RECORD the pinpointed lists and the agreement.

Set the CONSEQUENCES for violating the agreement.

Section Four

Applications to Problem Children

This section details, step by step, the application of social learning procedures for changing the behavior of young, aggressive children. Such children are characterized by any one of the following: (1) high rates of hitting siblings, peers, and/or parents; (2) high rates of noncompliance; or (3) high rates of teasing, yelling, or noisy behaviors. They are often also described as failing in school and as having difficulty with peers. Some of them set fires and steal. Many of them are described as "immature" and "hyperactive." Follow-up studies of such children indicate that their eventual adjustment as adults may be tenuous. [24] Even as adults they are likely to continue to have severe problems in their relationships to other people and to the world of work.

The material in this section summarizes five years' intensive research and clinical experience in working with families of aggressive boys.[10,13] The observation data collected in these homes prior to, during, and for twelve months following intervention suggest that approximately seventy percent of the parents were successful in changing the behavior of their children.[13] The parents of these boys were given extensive supervised training in the use of the principles outlined in this section.

About half of the boys also displayed severe problems in the classroom, including inability to get along with other children, failure in academic subjects, and high rates of fighting and noncompliance. The procedures for training the teacher and the peer group to alter the reinforcing contingencies for these children will not be described here, but have been presented in various technical reports.[13] While the parents serve key roles in treating these children, it does seem necessary in the case of such severe problems to collaborate with a professional person.

The earlier book, *Living with Children*, contained chapters describing procedures for working with withdrawn, dependent-immature, and fearful children. Since publishing that book, we have carried out no further clinical research; for this reason, no attempt was made to include chapters relevant to these problem areas in the present volume. Those interested in these problems should refer to the earlier volume.

This section would, of course, be *required* reading for parents who have children displaying high rates of one or more of the aggressive behaviors. It was, in fact, written explicitly for these parents. However, it also serves as a general example of planning and carrying out programs. The details of the steps involved and the overall continuity of the programs employed should give the average parent a more detailed account of how one goes about designing and carrying out intervention programs.

eleven

The Aggressive Child

"You just don't know when he is
going to blow up."
"He just keeps things stirred up all
the time."
"It is impossible to get him to do
anything."
"He is stubborn, just like his father."
"He acts as if no one likes him."
"He has a terrible temper."

What is *meant* by the phrase "aggressive
child"? Other children hit, tease, and they sometimes refuse to obey adult requests. Actually, the
aggressive child does what *most* children do, but *at
higher rates* and *in situations where it is not ac-
ceptable*. However, most children do *not* hit as
often as once a day; they do *not* tease at the rate
of once an hour. They obey most parental requests and demands. Hitting, noncompliance, and
"bugging" are behaviors displayed by most children sometimes; however, the aggressive child
distinguishes himself by displaying them at higher
(1) _____.

The aggressive child teases his younger
brother, hits, and yells in such a variety of

1. rates

settings that the parents become confused. "You just never know what he is going to do." He may have a temper outburst in the midst of an otherwise pleasant scene, such as a birthday party or at a store. He may tease his sister while on a shopping trip or noncomply in the presence of visitors. The aggressive child displays his high rate behaviors in a wider variety of (2) se_____ than do other children.

When such a pattern of high rate responding develops, it is likely to cause changes within the total family system. The brothers and sisters may get caught up in a pattern of using teasing, yelling, and hitting at high rates. The parents can also find themselves spanking more often. The children and the parents tend to label the aggressive child as "bad," and he comes to think of himself in this way. When asked why he does these things he cannot give an explanation; usually he blames others for forcing him to act in this way. "They bugged me so I had to hit 'em."

If a crisis arises, a displeasure occurs, or he is momentarily blocked from obtaining a reward, he attacks. With such a child (or adult) it is difficult to conceive of forming a close relationship. In the school he is avoided by other children. *He is disliked by other people.*[7] Not only does he inflict pain upon other people, but he tends not to reinforce other children or adults. It is indeed difficult to like such a person. For good reason, then, he *feels* that he is rejected and disliked, as indeed he is. It is an odd fact that in spite of his skill in disrupting a whole household or classroom, he is *not* very sure of himself! He teaches others to dislike him.

His attacks create a pervading unpleasant mood. He also creates a situation in which both parents and the siblings are changed. The brothers and sisters are provided with a highly skilled model for teasing, hitting, and noncompliance. In

2. settings

106

addition, they are placed in a learning situation where they must learn to retaliate in some manner. An attack increases the likelihood that at some time in the future the victim will retaliate. [19] If the older brother is hitting and teasing his younger sister, she will learn to return the attacks in some form. Then *two* persons are behaving in a manner which will disrupt the whole household. Unless the parents find some means of handling the attacks of the aggressive child, other children in the family will almost certainly devise means of retaliating. Attacks breed (3) at . The aggressive child will respond to these counterattacks with yet further attacks which escalate the conflicts within the home.

The adults within the family are also drawn into this escalating interchange. Even if they believe that it is "good" for boys to learn to fight and tease, they will find that the noise level exceeds their tolerance level. As the children increase their rates of attacks and counterattacks, the parents resort to yelling, nagging, and spanking. All of these will temporarily shut off the conflict. This slight interruption in chaos (4) _____ both parents for yelling, nagging, and spanking. We now have a situation in which the behavior of one person--the aggressive child--sets up a *chain reaction which eventually involves all members of the family*. The family is a social system in that what one person does influences what other members do.

As more family members get drawn into the conflict, making increasing use of zapping and punishment, they probably begin to develop feelings about the family which are increasingly negative. Also it is probably difficult to use positive social reinforcement with people who are making you miserable. This means that members of these families may end up being forced to use primarily

3. attacks   4. reinforces

painful consequences to control each other's behavior. At the end of such an escalating process, there is little "love" in such homes.

The reinforcer for aggressive behaviors is usually not praise, social approval, points, or money. Hitting is strengthened because it "works" in removing aversive stimuli. The process is similar to that which strengthens parental yelling, nagging, and scolding. The sister's teasing is an (5) _____ stimulus. The aggressive child has learned that if he hits her, it will (6)_____ her teasing. The behavior that is strengthened here is (7) _____ . This increases the likelihood that he will hit in the future. He learns that hitting "works" in turning off a wide variety of unpleasant situations. A family need only *allow* the hitter to be reinforced in this manner to produce a high rate of hitting. The same child usually learns that a temper tantrum is an effective means of training parents to stop asking him to do things he doesn't want to do.

Why do some families have high rate hitters and not others? While it may be that there are related genetic or physiological differences among children, there are as yet no studies which firmly establish these differences as "causing" aggressive behavior. On the other hand, it has been shown that an amazing variety of aggressive children can be trained to *stop hitting*. Retarded children, brain-damaged children, adolescents, and even autistic children can be trained to lower their hitting rates.

The parents of aggressive children do not necessarily have "psychiatric problems," nor are they "stupid" or "bad" people. Many of them have already reared several children very effectively. Parents of the aggressive child do have one thing in common, though; they do not provide consistent consequences for hitting or noncom-

5. aversive   6. stop   7. hitting

pliance. *Occasionally* they will punish hitting, teasing, or noncompliant behavior, but more often than not the behaviors are reinforced. Some parents have been told that their child is retarded, brain damaged, or emotionally disturbed, with the implication that limits and structure would be "bad" for the child. Some children have been cared for by baby sitters or grandparents who have provided no consequences for such behaviors. Some parents have simply been so busy with the world outside the family that they have not taken the time to track the child's behavior and provide consequences. The thing that they all have in common is that they do not track these hitting, teasing, and noncompliant behaviors, nor do they provide a (8)_____ when the behaviors occur.

Again, it should be stressed that these children are not born (9) _____ . They do not have something wrong with them. They have been TRAINED to be high rate hitters by members of their own (10) _____ . Parents from all walks of life can accidentally slip into the pattern which will produce this kind of training. Most importantly, the family *can* retrain such a child to (11) _____ his rates of hitting, teasing, and noncompliance.

This does not mean that the appropriate goal is necessarily that of teaching him *never* to hit. In our society, it *might* be necessary for him to be able to fight back when he is attacked. The goal, specifically, is to teach him to hit at a lower rate, and in appropriate situations.

8. punishment, consequence   9. bad
10. family   11. reduce

KEY IDEAS
High rate hitting, teasing, and noncompliance characterize the aggressive child.
Children and adults reject him.
These behaviors are learned.
They are reinforced because they remove unpleasant situations.
The aggressive child can learn to stop hitting.

twelve

Pinpointing and Changing Noncompliance

Each aggressive child seems to have learned a slightly different pattern of high rate behaviors. Some hit only their little brothers; others hit everyone, including their parents. Some tease, run away from school and home, steal, and light fires. Others are noisy and hyperactive, while others are silent and rather withdrawn. Each aggressive child is somewhat unique; and it is up to the family to pinpoint the specific problems which define the child's aggressive behaviors.

With these children it is wise to begin with *one* problem behavior at a time. DO NOT select the problem that "bothers you the most" as a point of beginning. Practice on relatively trivial problems first. It is also important to select a behavior that occurs at a fairly high rate, that is, at least once an hour. Learning to deal with this relatively simple problem requires that you practice the basic skills which will be used to deal with more complex aspects of aggression. "Noncompliance" is a good problem behavior for your first program. Noncompliance means that the parent makes a request and the child does not comply. Most aggressive children display high rates of these behaviors.

Each child has different ways of operating. You must observe your child for a day or two to see what his noncompliance technique is. For

111

example, he may be an "instant exploder." If asked to carry out the garbage, he responds with loud yells and informs the world that it is definitely not his turn. When does his sister do anything? People are always hassling him.

There is also the "smiling footdragger": in his most cheerful voice, "Sure, Mom, right away." Somehow the garbage does not get taken out right then, nor later. Unless his mother follows him about the house and nags, he just "forgets." Some of them are three-, four-, even eight-nag children. It depends upon how well they have trained their parents. A true maestro can get his parents up to ten nags *and still comply only once in a while!* They find it is easier to do it themselves than to try to out-nag him.

The request should be stated specifically: "I'd like the garbage taken out in the next thirty minutes." Specify the amount of (1) _____ he has to comply. If the child does not do it in the specified time, it is a noncomply. If you have to argue or ask him twice, it is a noncomply. If he is doing something he really enjoys, give him a time period in which to become disengaged: "As soon as that TV program is over, please take the garbage out." For some behaviors, you will not, of course, brook any delay: "Stop that teasing right now, both of you." If the teasing continues, that is a noncomply.

If the behavior occurs at a high rate (two or more times per hour), you might select just one or two hours each day during which you will make your count. During that time make sure that both parents give him several requests. If his noncomplies are less than once an hour, you might decide to count occurrences during the whole day. (2) _____ parents should participate in this counting. Some fathers attempt to gracefully bow out and "leave it to mother."

1. time   2. Both

Don't let this happen. Your program will almost certainly fail if both parents are not participating.

Take a data card from the appendix of this book and keep it in a spot that is easily accessible, i.e., the refrigerator door, or taped on the wall by the stove. Identify the specific behaviors which define noncompliance for your child.

DATA CARD					
NAME _Eric_			DATES _Dec 1_ to _Dec 5_		
BEHAVIOR: _Noncomply - argues when asked to do something, forgets to do it, refuses, takes too long to get it done, it is so sloppy it has to be done over._					
DAY	POINTS	FREQUENCY	TIME	RATE	COMMENTS
Mon		~~HHH~~ 11	3:30-4:30	.12 per min	
Tues		1	3:30-4:00	.03 per min	
Wed		~~HHH~~	3:30-4:20	.10 per min	
Thurs		~~HHH~~ 111	3:30 4:30	.13 per min	

Calculate your rate on the basis of hours or minutes; you may find the arithmetic is somewhat simpler when using minutes. In either case, Eric, the boy in the example above, is turning out high rates of noncompliant behavior. The parents should collect a baseline of at least (3) _____ days of data in order to obtain a stable starting point. In spite of the temptation to "get going," do not rush this phase.

This particular boy, Eric, was ten years of age and a practiced monster. He not only hit his younger sister, but had completely alienated himself from children in the neighborhood as well.

3. three

113

He was so bossy that other children avoided playing with him. He was likely to settle disagreements with an all-out attack. At home he made derogatory remarks about his mother and particularly his sister. He was large enough and aggressive enough so that his mother felt she could not handle him. The father claimed that he was well-behaved when he was home; observations in the home showed that this, in fact, was the case.

Eric was so skilled at noncompliance that neither the father nor the mother asked him to do anything. As is the case for most aggressive boys, both parents had been trained to believe that Eric could not mind or do chores. After four days of baseline observation it was clear that he provided about one noncomply every ten minutes. Even on his best day, which was (4)_____, his noncompliance rate was (5)_____ per minute. At the end of baseline the parents discussed the data with him and explained the contract.

"Eric, we have been counting your 'not minding' for the last few days." He hardly indicated that he had heard. "Ma, can I go outside now?" The father pointed at the chair and said, "You sit down for a minute, then you can go out." Then Eric, still standing, answered, "Why should I? Look at Lauri; she never does anything around here. Little six-year-old, doll-sister, never has to do anything. Why is she so special, anyhow?"

The mother avoided this sidetracking maneuver and stayed on the topic, "Starting right now we are going to help you practice minding. Lauri is going to practice not bugging

4. Tuesday   5. .03

114

you. I think you will find that programs are sort of fun; the way that they work is that you get a point each time you mind when your father or me asks you to do something. For example, if I say 'Please come to supper in the next couple of minutes,' and you do it, then you get a point. We keep track of the points right here." She points to the data card.

Eric is sitting staring out the window, as if he does not hear. His father is becoming slightly irritated at this, "You can earn points every day for doing what you are told. After a couple of days you can use the points to buy something that you want. What do you want to use the points for?" Eric quietly whispers, "I don't want no points for nothin'."

He refuses to negotiate. This has the desired effect of completely unraveling his father. Before the father can move in with his heavy artillery and "solve the problem," the mother continues.

"Well, you can decide what you would like to earn later. For now we will give you a nickel for each 'minding behavior'; we will keep the money in this jar and you can have whatever you earn at the end of the day. O.K., let's have one practice, to see if we all understand. This is for real; and you will earn a point and a nickel. Eric, please turn the TV set down for me before you go outside."

Eric slowly drags out of the room and touches the volume knob before going outside. His mother said, "O.K., that is a point," and puts a nickel in the jar. "Thank you, Eric."

115

In this discussion, Eric tried to sabotage the negotiations and direct the topic elsewhere. He did this by attacking Lauri and attempting to get the parents to defend the child management procedures they used with her. He also refused to negotiate the back-up reinforcers for the point program. Many aggressive children approach their first session in this manner. *Ignore the words* they use and attempt to immediately provide a reinforcer for whatever level of compliance you can get from them. In this case, Eric barely touched the volume knob, so his first response was hardly satisfactory by most standards. However, that is where he is at the present time. During the first day, even minimal compliance is reinforced.

Do not lecture when he noncomplies. Just record them and ignore them. Emphasize your pleasure at the minimal compliance you do obtain. If the problem is severe, "pay off" at the end of each day.

"Eric, here are the three nickels you earned today for minding. That was really nice when you set the table when I asked you. That is a help. What do you think you will earn tomorrow?"

After several days of using pennies or nickels, you might again raise the issue of what he would like to earn with his points and make several suggestions to him. Try to negotiate for natural consequences as soon as possible.

Both parents might select one hour during the day when they will search for and find some aspect of the child's behavior that can be reinforced. You might agree between yourselves as to what the target behaviors might be; they should, of course, include "comply," but also might include things like, "acting more grown-up," "being

116

less noisy," "being helpful," or "playing appropriately." During that hour try to dispense five to ten social reinforcers of different kinds for any of these behaviors. As reinforcers you might use (6)_____ ,(7)_____, (8)_____, or (9) _____.

After the reinforcement programs are underway, you are in a position to introduce TO for noncompliance. Carefully controlled laboratory research has shown that for many aggressive children it is necessary to supplement the effects of reinforcement by the use of TO.[29,30] Many parents hesitate to introduce it for retraining their aggressive child because they are afraid that they cannot follow through in carrying it out. However, it is an important aspect of the training program.

"Eric, you have been doing pretty well on the program, but you still forget to mind. We are going to start using Time Out to help you remember. It will also help your father and me to stop nagging and scolding as much as we do. From now on, if you forget to mind when I ask you to do something, then you go to Time Out. That means that you go and sit in the bathroom for five minutes. When we tell you to go in, we will set the timer for five minutes. When the timer goes off, you can come out."

Eric is scowling at this point, "Go ahead and put me in there; I like to be away from all you creeps, anyway. I like to be by myself. I like it in the toilet. Go on, put me in

6, 7, 8, 9. Might include any of the following: praise, approval, smile, touch, caress, kiss, attention, participating in what he is doing

there right now, see if I care! It ain't going to work."

The mother ignores this and goes on, "If you come out before the timer goes off, you have to stay in one minute extra. Or if you talk to anyone while you are in there, that costs an extra minute, too."

Eric does not look at her or his father, "Aw, what a crummy thing. Just like a jail. What about Lauri, huh? What about her? Does she go in there too?"

But remember to use **TO** (10)_____ time the noncompliance occurs. When Eric was jumping up and down on the couch an hour later, his father told him to go to **TO**, and then set the timer for five minutes.

Eric ran outside and stood on the sidewalk, yelling at his father, "I ain't going in there; I'm going to run away. It's just a crummy jail in that house!"

The father was getting angry, but said, "That is one minute extra for running out here. It is another minute for yelling at me. You'd better come in and get it over with. It is another minute for each one that you stay out here." With that, he closed the door and went back into the house.

Eric circled the house for a few minutes, occasionally stopped to make a face in the window, but eventually came in. "O.K. Five minutes, that's all. Besides, I like it in there."

10. every

118

His father announced, "No, it is not five minutes; you were outside for eight minutes, you have an extra minute for yelling at me, one for running outside, and three for making faces through the window. That is eighteen altogether."

Eric began to yell and kick at the door as he went in. His father closed the door and said calmly, "That is one more for yelling and another for kicking the door."

When Eric had been in there a few minutes, he began to shout, "Is it time yet?" When no one answered, he began to cry. At this point his mother became upset and stated loudly enough for Eric to hear that perhaps he should be let out. A short time later he burst out of the bathroom and announced that he was all through. The father returned him to TO and added an additional minute. Each yell that followed cost him more time, but the father no longer announced each one. When, at the end of thirty minutes, he came out, the father told him, again, that each yell, kick, and running out of the room had cost him. Some parents find it necessary to actually hold the door the first few times. If this happens, make sure you do not talk to the child while he is in TO.

By the end of the first week the combination of TO with the point program and social reinforcement seemed to be having some effect. Both parents reported that things were changing in that home was now *occasionally* pleasant. Surprisingly enough, Eric acted as if he were happier!

The point programs were changed several times so that by the second week he was working for five or six days in order to earn the fifty points necessary for his father to take him trout fishing. The trip was a huge success. The father had previously noted his tendency to criticize

Eric in all kinds of situations and made a special effort to keep these comments in check. He found Eric to be genuinely interested in learning some of the myriad skills necessary to become a trout fisherman. While other trips were planned, Eric next elected to earn one hundred points for an inexpensive secondhand TV set for his room. Interestingly enough, the parents found that as the programs progressed they began asking Eric to assume more responsibilities about the house, including sharing in the dishwashing in the evenings. Eric shared the responsibility with his mother for one week and Lauri did them the following week. The general progress is described in the figure below.

FIGURE 2
ERIC'S NONCOMPLIANCE

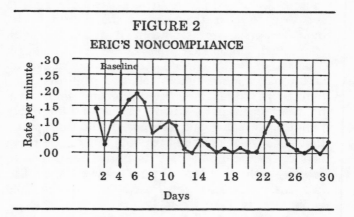

As the figure shows, the first week produced no change; in fact, the first (11)_____ days of data looked *worse* than the baseline. It is also clear that Eric is far from being perfect; but then again, the parents did not require this of him. On the eighteenth day of training the grandparents arrived for the holidays. Both of them

11. three

objected to the use of TO and points. Their contribution to the family is recorded on the graph.

At the end of the second week, the parents felt that things were going well enough to consider beginning new programs. These are described in the chapter that follows.

KEY IDEAS
The parents pinpoint the specific aggressive behavior of their child.
Only one relatively trivial problem behavior should be selected at the beginning of the program.
Noncompliance is an appropriate problem behavior for the first program.
The request for compliance should be stated specifically.
Both parents must participate in the program.
During the first day, even minimal compliance is reinforced.
After the reinforcement program is underway, TO is introduced for noncompliance.

thirteen

Changing Other Aggressive Behaviors

Things got a little better with Eric. After having been successful with the noncompliance program, his parents were slightly encouraged. At least they proved to themselves that they really could help Eric change his behavior. However, it was also clear that the most difficult problems still remained. He and Lauri were constantly bugging and teasing each other; major battles occurred several times a day. Some of these battles got the whole family embroiled, and bad feelings remained for hours afterward. He seemed to go out of his way to make everyone uncomfortable. For example, he would stand behind his mother as she was talking to someone, making like a metronome, saying "Mom, Mom, Mom, Mom, Mom ..." until she stopped what she was doing and and responded to him. He would still explode and throw things or hit without warning at home and in the school and the neighborhood. These explosions earned him the label of "dangerous" by other parents and by teachers. Many of the families in the neighborhood would not allow their children to play with Eric.

About half of the children who show high rates of aggressive behaviors and noncompliance at home have problems at school of a similar order. Eric was no exception. Even though he was in the second grade, he was reading at an early first-grade level. He was constantly disrupting the class -- clowning around, running about the room, and laughing and talking in a loud voice to his neighbors. When asked to do something by the teacher, he was very likely to ignore her or talk back to her. He would seldom complete his assignments, and when he did, the work was sloppy and, very likely, incorrect. Once every week or so he would have an explosion in which he would attack other children with anything at hand. The danger to the other children understandably frightened his teachers.

Eric's behavior is only part of this problem. His little sister Lauri is an important piece to this puzzle. She had an uncanny knack of knowing just what buttons to push to set her brother off. While things might start out as "play," it is amazing how often games turned into arguments, running shaded into pushing, and teasing led to hitting. Certainly it cannot be said that Lauri "started" all of these battles. It is just that she was a necessary component for most of them. Extensive observations made in homes of both problem and non-problem families show that this is not unusual. The member of the family most likely to trigger aggressive behaviors is the younger sister or younger brother.[10] Lauri was an attractive young lady, four years of age, already practiced in the feminine wiles necessary to stop her father in mid-stride. By saying something cute and delivering an impish grin, she could interrupt her father in the middle of his saying "no," and cause him to forget what he was trying to do. Because she was so young, the parents were reluctant to involve her in a training program. After all, she was only four, and "their last baby."

While it was conceivable that Eric's behavior could be changed without directly changing Lauri's, it would have been inefficient--clumsy and time consuming--especially since Lauri would have had to learn some other means of relating to her brother eventually. Certainly from Eric's viewpoint, justice would be better served by a program which did something about this younger sister, who was always bugging him.

The next step involved setting up a dual contract which would apply both to Eric and Lauri.

The first contract did not involve any of the school problems, but did identify the high points in the problems to be found at home. An effort was made to find those behaviors that would apply to both Eric and Lauri and also to find back-up reinforcers appropriate to both.

Each time that Eric or Lauri was pleasant, the parents would label the behavior, "That's nice. You two are playing well together. You both get a point." The mother would then walk over and put a mark in the box for each child. Neither Eric nor Lauri could completely dress themselves. They had trained their mother to believe that they both were completely helpless. While the mother still laid out their clothes for them, she made an extra effort to be very reinforcing if they made any moves to dress themselves. In the first session with Eric, he managed to get his pants and shirt on by himself, and the mother promptly reinforced this: "That's very good, Eric; you get one point for that." She also made similar evaluations for the way in which the two children made their beds on the first few days. In fact, on the first day neither child made the bed nor cleaned up the room. The mother commented as she walked down the hall that nobody got any points today because the room was still a mess and neither bed had been made. Lauri seized upon this opportunity to do her brother one better and quickly shoved clothes and toys under the bed and draped the bedcover over the sheets and blankets underneath. The mother later commented that she got one-half point for trying to clean up her room and the next time she could get even more by putting the dirty clothes away, hanging her clothes up, and taking a little more time in making the bed.

124

CONTRACT FOR ERIC AND LAURI Dates_____		M	T	W	T	F	S	S
BEHAVIOR		M	T	W	T	F	S	S
PLEASANT +1	ERIC							
	LAURI							
GET DRESSED BY SELF +2	ERIC							
	LAURI							
MAKE BED CLEAN ROOM +3	ERIC							
	LAURI							
MIND PARENTS +1	ERIC							
	LAURI							
ASK TO LEAVE +2	ERIC							
	LAURI							
DO CHORES +4	ERIC							
	LAURI							
TEASE, BUG, YELL -2	ERIC							
	LAURI							
HIT, GRAB, SHOVE -3	ERIC							
	LAURI							
NOT MIND -1	ERIC							
	LAURI							
BREAK, TEAR THINGS -2	ERIC							
	LAURI							
TOTAL	ERIC							
TOTAL	LAURI							

Tease, yell, bug, hit, grab, shove, or not mind means five minutes TO.
+3 points, get special treat for afternoon snack.
+5 points, may use bike and leave yard.
+7 points, can stay up 30 minutes longer (15 minutes for Lauri).

Both children were in the habit of simply wandering off through the neighborhood and seldom, if ever, letting the parents know where they were going. On the first day of the contract, a very short practice session was held, in which each child practiced telling their mother and father that they were going somewhere. Both of the parents also practiced reinforcing them for doing this.

When the contract was first 'explained to them, neither child really understood all of the complexities involved. Lauri, of course, could not follow all the business with numbers and points. She did, however, understand that in the future, teasing, bugging, yelling, hitting, and so forth would lead to Time Out for herself and for Eric, because in the past week she had seen this consequence applied. She also had a vague notion that if she worked hard, she could get more points than Eric and maybe get an afternoon treat and stay up later. Within two or three days, both children understood the details of the contract very well. Each time one of the listed behaviors occurred, it was labeled by the parents, who then immediately walked over and placed an appropriate mark on the contract. The relationship between their behavior and scores then became readily apparent.

Both parents wore wrist counters for the first week in order to keep track of the social reinforcers that they were using. Each of them attempted to provide fifteen reinforcers for each child each day. This, of course, was not always possible, because occasionally the father would come home late and there would be little opportunity to reinforce Lauri, who was in bed by 7:30 p.m.

Each day when Eric returned from school at 2:30 the mother would total the point scores for both children and decide whether or not they had earned their special treat. Actually, the special treat for the first few weeks consisted of an assortment of candy bars. This back-up reinforcer proved to be something highly prized by both children. Adding up the points at this time often led to a flurry of "good behaviors," as the children wanted to build up points in order to earn the right to leave the yard and play in the neighborhood. In Eric's case, it was necessary to keep his bike chained in the garage during the first week. On the first occasion of being told that he had not earned enough points for his bike, he simply slipped out of the house, removed his bicycle and was gone for two hours. This was not covered in the contract, but he lost his TV privileges for that evening. The next day his father bought a chain and padlock for the bike. The idea of earning anything was totally new to Eric.

Most aggressive children do not do chores. To Eric and Lauri's parents, it seemed easier to do the chores themselves than to supervise the children while they did what was, at best, an inadequate job. However, eventually it was decided that Lauri should pick up in the living room each day--putting magazines away, emptying ashtrays, and so forth. Eric was to clear the dishes from the table in the evening and stack them on the counter by the sink. During the first week, neither of them earned a full point for their chores.

After the first week or two, both children became thoroughly familiar with the point concept and it was then possible to make arrangements for long-term contracts. It was agreed, for example, that when both children had earned forty points, they would be accompanied by one of the parents to a Saturday matinee movie. Later still, they earned points for a one-day trip to the coast.

Over a period of weeks the contracts were changed many times. New behaviors were added and old ones deleted. The general progress of Eric's programs are noted in Figure 3.

As the data show, Eric had his ups and downs--periodically he would have stormy periods when he seemed very much like his old self again. His general pattern of improvement, with the sharp peaks and valleys, is fairly characteristic. A graph for Lauri would look similar to this. As

127

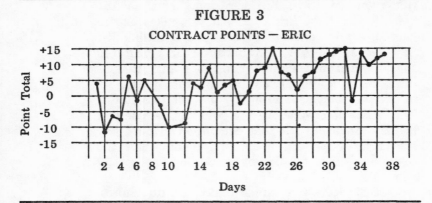

FIGURE 3

CONTRACT POINTS — ERIC

could be expected, after a period of several weeks Eric generally became more predictable and consistent in what he did. The point is quickly reached where the child almost always can be expected to be reasonable and to behave himself. Interestingly enough, as these improvements occurred, Eric also became more affectionate. He was able to touch people without mauling them, to sit with his mother without acting silly, and occasionally to volunteer doing something nice for another family member. It was possible to leave the children with a baby sitter. Even more unusual was the fact that the same baby sitter was willing to return for further engagements.

By the fourth and fifth weeks of the program several neighbors had spontaneously commented to the mother that Eric seemed to be behaving differently now. This is not to say that at this point Eric was a likeable child; he still would be characterized, at best, as "immature." As the aggressive behaviors came under control, the parents shifted the focus of the program to concentrate on reinforcing him for more mature behaviors. Also, the general tone of family interaction had undergone subtle changes by this point. The father commented that he no longer needed some special preparation in order to walk into his own home after work in the evening. The noise level had fallen appreciably, and the crisis rate diminished dramatically. The parents and children had, for the first time, begun to make plans about activities that the family could engage in together on weekends.

When it was apparent that the programs being carried out by the parents were partially effective, the school was contacted to determine the possibility of working with Eric in the classroom. The principal and teacher were willing to permit both the collection of observation data in the classroom and also the application of the intervention procedures which had been designed particularly for that purpose. [12,23]

Baseline observations in the classroom showed that Eric was spending only thirty percent of his time working on school material in contrast to the other children, who spent approximately seventy percent of their time "on task." He spent an inordinate amount of time roaming about the classroom teasing and disrupting other children. When asked by the teacher to sit down or to carry out an assignment, he would typically noncomply and become obviously angry as she pushed the point. He was also observed destroying paper and pencils and cutting deep marks into his desk top.

One of the first negotiations involved a contingency for Eric's attacking another child or displaying a severe temper tantrum in the classroom. He was to be taken to the principal's office and required to call his parents. His mother would come to school and take him home, where he would be required to scrub the bathroom, and then promptly return to school.

A small card was scotch-taped to Eric's desk each morning. (See the sample card on page 130.) On the first few days of its use, the teacher walked by Eric's desk every five or ten minutes and assigned him points on the basis of the behavior she observed during that time. For example, if he had been sitting at his desk, he could earn three points. If he had been working during that

ERIC	DATE _____
SITTING AT DESK (3)	
WORKING (3)	
NEATNESS AND ACCURACY (3)	
NO TEASING OR HITTING (3)	
TOTAL	

time, he might earn another three points. He could also earn points for being neat, accurate, and not disrupting other children. On the first day, the teacher announced to the class that if Eric could earn a full thirty points that morning, they would get out five minutes early for recess. To the delight of all the other children in the group, Eric met that contract and with great pride brought his desk card home that night.

An item was also added to the parents' contract so that he received additional points at home for points earned at school. In this manner the school and the family were working together to provide a supportive program for Eric.

Actually, during the first three weeks of the school program, it was necessary for the mother to "run and fetch" Eric only once. On that particular day, the teacher mentioned that he had seemed to come to school with a chip on his shoulder. He scowled fiercely when asked to do perfectly ordinary things, and quickly lost a number of points for pushing and teasing other children. Later that morning, he tipped his desk over and threw his books about the room. He was quickly removed from the room and taken to the principal's office. After ten minutes of sitting, he made the telephone call to his mother, which resulted in a thirty-minute session of scrubbing the bathroom.

As the classroom program took effect, Eric spent more time working at his seat, and his work increased dramatically in accuracy and neatness. Arrangements were also made for one of the other children to work with him as he went through programmed materials in arithmetic and reading. Because he was essentially two years behind in his academic work at this point, it was deemed necessary to set up a special summer program for him. In this six-weeks' program, Eric concentrated on reading and arithmetic skills along with a group of children who were having similar problems. The parents were also given special training in using comparable materials. Very short, daily practice sessions were held in the home after the parents had received supervision by Karl Skindrud.[25] The program placed a heavy emphasis upon both social reinforcers and points earned for accurate behavior. Six months after the beginning of this classroom intervention program, Eric had accelerated a year and a half in his reading skills and was an accepted member of his peer group in that school. When asked about Eric the following year, his new teacher said that he was no particular problem, but she had other boys in the class who were in need of assistance.

Certainly Eric behaves differently now, in both the home and the school. This is not to say that he never hits or pushes or teases; he still does all of these things. What has changed is the rate with which he does them, and the settings in which he's likely to use them. If another child attacks him, Eric will fight back. Certainly, he still teases his sister Lauri once in a while. He is not a perfect child, but now he is pleasant to be around. He is a human being with whom it is now possible to live. And, his parents say that he is now possible to love.

KEY IDEAS

The aggressive child's brothers and sisters should be included in the program.

The children should be taught to do and be given points for chores.

Children who do not comply at home often have the same problem at school.

The classroom teacher can use a program similar to that of the parents'.

Additional points can be given at home for points earned at school.

References

1. Bandura, A., and Walters, R.H. *Social learning and personality development.* New York: Holt, Rinehart & Winston, 1963.

2. Ebner, M. Personal communication, 1970.

3. Homans, G.C. *Social behavior: Its elementary forms.* New York: Harcourt, Brace & World, 1961.

4. Homme, L., with Csanyi, A.P., Gonzales, M.A., and Rechs, J. R. *How to use contingency contracting in the classroom.* Champaign, Ill.: Research Press, 1970.

5. Lederer, W.J. and Jackson, D.D. *The mirages of marriage.* New York: Norton, 1968.

6. Lindsley, O.R. Personal communication, 1970.

7. Moore, S. Correlates of peer acceptance in nursery school children. *Young Children,* 1967, *22,* 281-297.

8. Morris, H.H. Aggressive behavior disorders in children: A follow-up study. *American Journal of Psychiatry,* 1956, *112,* 991-997.

9. Patterson, G.R. Behavioral techniques based upon social learning: An additional base for developing behavior modification technologies. In C.M. Franks (Ed.), *Behavior therapy: Appraisal and status.* New York: McGraw-Hill, 1969. Pp. 341-374.

10. Patterson, G.R. and Cobb, J.A. A dyadic analysis of "aggressive" behaviors: An additional step toward a theory of aggression. In J.P. Hill (Ed.), *Minnesota Symposia on Child Psychology.* Vol. 5. Minneapolis: University of Minnesota Press, 1971, in press.

11. Patterson, G.R. and Cobb, J.A. The structure of aggressive behavior. In J.F. Knutson (Ed.), *Iowa symposium on the control of aggression.* Iowa City: University of Iowa Press, 1971, in press.

12. Patterson, G.R., Cobb, J.A., and Ray, R.S. Direct intervention in the classroom. In F. Clark, D. Evans, and L. Hamerlynck (Eds.), *Behavior Technology for Education.* Calgary, Alberta, Canada: University of Calgary Press, 1971, in press.

13. Patterson, G.R., Cobb, J.A., and Ray, R.S. A social engineering technology for retraining the families of aggressive boys. Paper presented at the Georgia Symposium in Experimental Clinical Psychology, University of Georgia, May 1970.

14. Patterson, G.R. and Gullion, M.E. *Living with children: New methods for parents and teachers.* Champaign, Ill.: Research Press, 1968.

15. Patterson, G.R. and Hops, H. Coercion, a game for two: Intervention techniques for marital conflict. In R.E. Ulrich and P. Mountjoy (Eds.), *The experimental analysis of social behavior.* New York: Appleton-Century-Crofts, 1972, in press.

16. Patterson, G.R., Littman, R.A., and Bricker, W. Assertive behavior in children: A step toward a theory of aggression. *Monographs of the Society for Research in Child Development,* 1967, *32,* No. 5, (Serial No. 113).

17. Patterson, G.R., McNeal, S., Hawkins, N., and Phelps, R. Reprogramming the social environment. *Journal of Child Psychology and Psychiatry,* 1967, *8,* 181-195. [Also in: R. Ulrich, T. Stachnick, and J. Mabry (Eds.), *Control of human behavior.* Vol. II. Glenview. Ill.: Scott, Foresman, 1970. Pp. 237-248.]

18. Patterson, G. R., Ray, R. S., and Shaw, D. A. Direct intervention in families of deviant children. *Oregon Research Institute Research Bulletin,* 1968, *8,* No. 9.

19. Patterson, G.R. and Reid, J.B. Reciprocity and coercion: Two facets of social systems. In C. Neuringer and J. Michael (Eds.), *Behavior modification in clinical psychology.* New York: Appleton-Century-Crofts, 1970. Pp. 133-177.

20. Patterson, G.R., Shaw, D.A., and Ebner, M.J. Teachers, peers, and parents as agents of change in the classroom. In F.A.M. Benson (Ed.), *Modifying deviant social behaviors in various classroom settings..* Eugene, Oreg.: University of Oregon, 1969, No. 1. Pp. 13-47.

21. Patterson, G.R. and White, G.D. It's a small world: The application of "Time-Out from positive reinforcement." *Oregon Psychological Association Newsletter,* 1969, *15,* 2, Supplement.

22. Phillips, E.L. and Wolf, M. Modification of behavioral deficiencies in adolescents. Paper presented at the American Psychological Association, San Francisco, 1968.

23. Ray, R.S., Shaw, D.A., and Cobb, J.A. The Work Box: An innovation in teaching attentional behavior. *The School Counselor,* 1970, *18,* 15-35.

24. Robins, L.N. *Deviant children grown up: A sociological and psychiatric study of sociopathic personality.* Baltimore: Williams & Wilkins, 1966.

25. Skindrud, K. Training mothers of disruptive nonreaders in remedial skills: A preliminary study of a home tutoring program. Unpublished manuscript, Oregon Research Institute, Eugene, 1971.

26. Skinner, B.F. *Science and human behavior.* New York: Appleton-Century-Crofts, 1953.

27. Stuart, R.B. Operant interpersonal treatment for marital discord. *Journal of Consulting and Clinical Psychology,* 1969, *33,* 675-682.

28. Ullmann, L.P. and Krasner, L. *A psychological approach to abnormal behavior.* Englewood Cliffs, N.J.; Prentice Hall, 1969.

29. Wahler, R.G. Behavior therapy with oppositional children: Attempts to increase their parents' reinforcement value. Paper presented at the meeting of the Southeastern Psychological Association, Atlanta, April 1967.

30. Walker, H.M., Mattson, R.H., and Buckley, N.K. Special class placement as a treatment alternative for deviant behavior in children. In F.A.M. Benson (Ed.), *Modifying deviant social behaviors in various classroom settings.* Eugene, Oreg.: University of Oregon Department of Special Education, 1969.

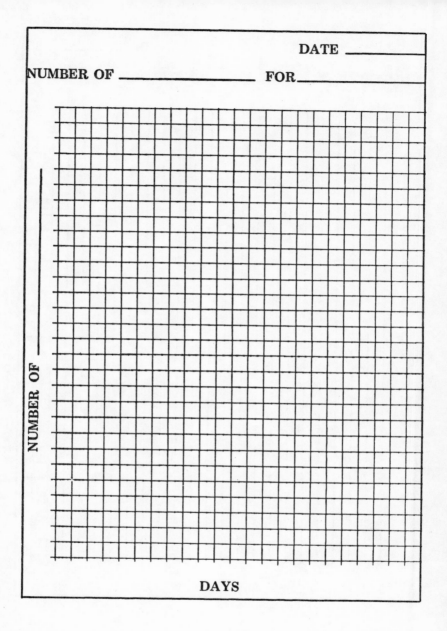

DATE _____

NUMBER OF _____ FOR_____

NUMBER OF _____

DAYS

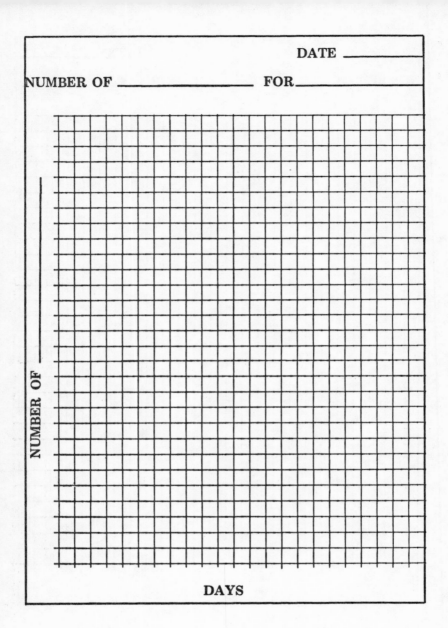

DATE _____

NUMBER OF _____ FOR_____

NUMBER OF _____

DAYS

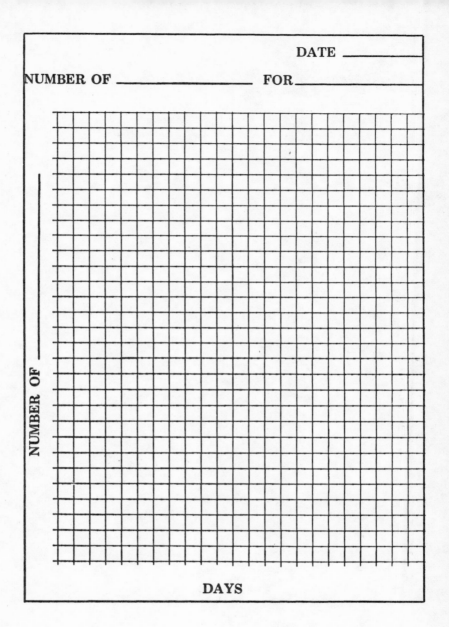

DATE _____

NUMBER OF _____ FOR_____

NUMBER OF

DAYS

DATA CARD

NAME _____ DATES _____ to _____

BEHAVIOR: _____

_____

DAYS	POINTS	FREQUENCY	TIME	RATE	COMMENTS

DATA CARD

NAME _____ DATES _____ to _____

BEHAVIOR: _____

DAYS	POINTS	FREQUENCY	TIME	RATE	COMMENTS

DATA CARD

NAME ——————— DATES ——— to ———

BEHAVIOR: ———————

DAYS	POINTS	FREQUENCY	TIME	RATE	COMMENTS